Department of Early Education and Care
Early Childhood Resource Center
Falmouth Public Library

Early Childhood Education

History, Theory, and Practice

Harry Morgan

ROWMAN & LITTLEFIELD EDUCATION.
Lanham • New York • Toronto • Plymouth, UK

Published in the United States of America
by Rowman & Littlefield Education
A Division of Rowman & Littlefield Publishers, Inc.
A wholly owned subsidary of The Rowman & Littlefield Publishing Group, Inc.
4501 Forbes Boulevard, Suite 200, Lanham, Maryland 20706
www.rowmaneducation.com

Estover Road
Plymouth PL6 7PY
United Kingdom

British Library Cataloguing in Publication Information Available

Library of Congress Cataloging-in-Publication Data

Morgan, Harry, 1926-
  Early childhood education : history, theory, and practice / Harry Morgan.
      p. cm.
  Includes bibliographical references and index.
  ISBN-13: 978-1-57886-502-4 (cloth : alk. paper)
  ISBN-10: 1-57886-502-6 (cloth : alk. paper)
  ISBN-13: 978-1-57886-503-1 (pbk. : alk. paper)
  ISBN-10: 1-57886-503-4 (pbk. : alk. paper)
  1. Early childhood education—United States. I. Title.
  LB1139.25.M64 2006
  372.210973—dc22   2006015220

$\bigcirc^{TM}$ The paper used in this publication meets the minimum requirements of American
National Standard for Information Sciences—Permanence of Paper for Printed Library
Materials, ANSI/NISO Z39.48-1992.
Manufactured in the United States of America.

Contents

Preface

EARLY CHILDHOOD EDUCATION:
HISTORY, THEORY, AND PRACTICE

The scope of this work includes the *history, theory, and practices* that have become professionally recognized and accepted as essential in studies of Early Childhood Education and Development. Historically, a variety of programs of study have been included under the title of Early Childhood Education. This variety includes preprimary education, nursery school, preschool, kindergarten, daycare, and child care, just to name a few. The transition from a life sheltered within family to one of daily classroom activities with others is one of the most critical steps in our lives as young children.

As states move to ensure basic standards like safety and space utilization, compliance is enforced through licensing of facilities according to the ages of children served. The designation of specific licensing by the age of children being served has in part contributed to the variety of program labels. Despite this variety, the age range of children included in early-childhood education extends from birth through age eight.

This book will discuss this age group from a variety of perspectives, including the lives of significant persons who influenced infant education and brought kindergarten to public schools. A history of these individuals, together with their theories and practices, will be explored, along with how their work has influenced early-childhood education and development as we know it today.

This writing will also take into account the needs and interests of university faculties who educate and supervise undergraduate and graduate students in the field and certified teachers who study the growth, development, and care of children from birth through eight years of age. Informed parents and home schoolers who invest their skills in supporting the educational needs of their own children will also find this book helpful.

The *practice* of early-childhood education is a human service. All human-service professionals, whether they are *educators, trainers, or classroom teachers,* perform their service from *philosophical* and *theoretical* perspectives. Practitioners and home-schooling caretakers should be knowledgeable about their *philosophy* because it is reflected in their performance and interactions with learners. Our philosophy serves as the foundation for our approach to work, and our practice is influenced by our values. As a teacher's approach to work is influenced by a teacher's *values,* this is referred to as a *hidden curriculum.*

Practitioners are also influenced by *theories* that they have acquired from observations and interactions with learners, professionals, and peers in their professional education. In this book, *theory* refers to empirical concepts that can be objectively observed and measured. It is a combination of our *philosophical* and *theoretical* influences that makes us the kind of *practitioners* that we become.

As early as Plato, schooling for young children was not thought useful until the child reached six years of age. It was believed that the child's needs up to this age should be met by family. It was not until the seventeenth century that philosophers and theorists like John Comenius viewed teaching and learning as essential for young children. Comenius thought that this task should be taken on by mothers and fathers. The organization of schooling for children under six did not occur until the eighteenth century through the work of Johann Oberlin in France and Johann Pestalozzi in Switzerland.

Early education centers called *Nursery Schools* were established in the United States primarily as child-development research laboratories in home economics departments for the education of teachers on university campuses. The first public nursery school was established in New York City in 1919, through a division of the *Bureau of Education Experiments* by Lucy Sprague Mitchell and Harriet Johnson. Mitchell and Johnson were also among the founders of a new college of education and child guidance intended for early-childhood teacher training, *Bank Street College.* Teacher's College of Columbia University and Merrill Palmer Institute in Detroit, Michigan, established nursery-school programs in 1922.

The education of children as young as two years old started as a European idea through the work of John Comenius, in Czechoslovakia; Johann Frederich Oberlin, in France; Robert Owen, in Scotland; Johann Heinrich Pestalozzi, in Switzerland; and Friedrich Froebel, in Germany.

In the United States, kindergarten started in the late 1800s primarily through the influence of Friedrich Froebel's students and *Transcendentalist* influences in the United States, which promoted the rights of children, the human rights of Native Americans, and freedom movements of African Americans held in slavery. Kindergarten, as a name for early education, originated with Froebel, and by the late 1800s the kindergarten idea was experiencing rapid growth in the United States.

It would be reasonable to start a history of early-childhood education with the kindergarten movement in the United States by noting that Margarethe Schurz, a German émigrée, opened the *first* U.S. kindergarten in Wisconsin. It was a small kindergarten conducted in the *German language* with Schurz's children as its first students.

One can also accurately point out that the first kindergarten in the United States was founded in Boston, Massachusetts, by Elizabeth Peabody in 1860, because it *was* the *first* kindergarten that was *taught in English*; despite the fact that it opened sometime after Schurz's.

Margarethe Schurz, as a student of Froebel, was encouraged by him to immigrate to the United States to promote the kindergarten idea, and she did just that. She introduced Peabody to the concept of kindergartens and encouraged her to read *The Education of Man*, the writings of Froebel (1887) describing his theory and philosophy of child growth and development through kindergarten education.

To start a historical discussion of kindergarten that highlighted the works of Schurz and Peabody might obscure the fact that in a French mining community, Johann Frederich Oberlin opened a school for children under the age of six in 1767, long before Froebel gave us the term *kindergarten*.

In the late 1700s, working toward the same goal, an organized movement for the education of children under the age of six was started in Europe, primarily through the work of Johann Heinrich Pestalozzi and Friedrich Froebel. In 1774, Pestalozzi converted his farm into a school for children from poor families where a young Froebel eventually became one of Pestalozzi's teachers.

Froebel's model was introduced in the United States through the initiatives of organizers like Margarethe Schurz and Elizabeth Peabody, who had studied with Froebel at different times in their lives. Peabody had not heard about kindergartens until she met Schurz. Both women in today's parlance would be labeled *liberals*.

Following her first attempts at operating a kindergarten, Peabody went to Europe for the specific purpose of studying with Froebel. Froebel formulated many of his ideas while working as a teacher in Pestalozzi's school for young children.

Peabody's attraction to kindergarten occurred somewhat late in life, during social and intellectual relationships with a scholarly group of philosophers in New England who were known collectively as *Transcendentalists.* Antislavery activism, as well as advocacy for human rights for Native Americans and equal rights for women were critical issues on the agenda of this notable group of well-known writers.

Some were attracted to this group out of scholarly curiosity and the desire to be in the company of poets and writers, while others, like Peabody, for example, were committed to social change and the philosophical and political beliefs of Transcendentalists everywhere.

The education of young children was a new and exciting movement that naturally attracted the Transcendentalists. Members in this group included Horace Mann, the famous early educator who married Peabody's sister Mary; Henry Bernard; Bronson Alcott; William E. Channing; Ralph Waldo Emerson, an acclaimed poet; Nathaniel Hawthorne, notable writer; and Henry David Thoreau, well known for his civil disobedience.

A Harvard graduate, Thoreau moved into a cabin near Concord, Massachusetts, where he lived alone for two years. With physical needs reduced to food and warmth that could be acquired in that environment, Thoreau lived close to Walden Pond and wrote about his quiet experiences. I suspect that Thoreau, from the quiet boundary of Walden, peered unnoticed down into a local community of folk because he needed a group of humans *to be away from* (1968).

The notables in this movement gave talks, speeches, and presentations at bookstores, garden societies, and Transcendentalist gatherings. Many of these gatherings took place in the homes of philanthropists, community notables, and other influential townsfolk. It was during these events that ideas of preschool education were spread. Bronson Alcott, the father of the famous writer Louisa May Alcott, opened a school for children in Massachusetts and hired Elizabeth Peabody as his assistant to advance the Transcendentalist influence in childhood education.

Public speeches attracted adherents and supporters to groups supporting women's rights, antislavery activism, Native American rights, and the kindergarten movement. General public support was slow in coming because the acceptance of public schools for children under six years of age meant higher taxes in communities where such schooling was accepted.

Despite this inevitability, Susan Blow, a Froebel-educated kindergartner, along with Elizabeth Peabody, convinced William T. Harris, superintendent of the St. Louis, Missouri, public schools, that his city should add kindergarten education to its regular school system. Harris opened the first public school kindergartens in the United States in 1873, and Susan Blow was among their first teachers. Other major cities followed, slowly.

Prior to an acceptance of kindergarten education in the United States as public policy, a period of uncertainty existed in the preschool education and care professions. At a time when few adults were trained to educate children under the age of six, the common query was, "Why would anyone need special training to teach the little ones?"

This was also a period before child labor laws, when there existed widespread mistreatment of young children required to work long hours on farms and in factories for the ultimate benefit of adults in their own families and for factory and farm owners.

In the late 1800s, following the tradition of Robert Owen, nursery schools for poor children were being organized in London and *kindergartners* (a name given teachers and supporters of the movement) in the United States took note of this development. Margaret McMillan in England brought to her position on the Bradford School Board an interest in the health of London's poor children, whose living conditions had not changed substantially since their depiction in Charles Dickens's novels.

Driven by this concern, Margaret and her sister Rachel founded a day and night nursery school for children ages one to six. Their social concerns included child labor practices, the system of care and placement of orphans, and education for young children.

In the United States, few teachers of children in this age group were well trained; services were also poor or inaccessible. Societies with a mission of organizing "nursery school" and "Bible school" groups struggled for a membership and an inclusive focus. These problems existed to some extent because there were nonspecific ways in which programs serving young children were identified and therefore confusing to the general population.

Such identifications were sometimes related to the age of the population being served, while at other times programs were identified by the type of service they provided (Bible school, for example).

In 1896, John Dewey and his wife founded a laboratory school at the University of Chicago for young children that ran for eight years. By 1920, there were over 150 kindergartens in public schools in the United States. Alice Temple, associate professor of kindergarten and primary education at the University of Chicago, and S. C. Parker, professor of educational methods at the University of Chicago, had been working for some time on a planned merger of kindergarten and first grade.

In the early 1920s the University of Chicago's School of Education, under the leadership of Professor Alice Temple, made the move to integrate curriculum for Froebel-educated kindergarteners with that of Chicago University's elementary-education teacher-training program. This integration served as a foundation for a University of Chicago teacher-training initiative and attracted the attention of Chicago's public school authorities, where kindergartens had been opened in ten schools by 1890.

Prior to the 1920s, university-level teacher-training programs offered undergraduate students one general curriculum for training as elementary school teachers, and a lesser alternative within this single curriculum for *kindergartners*. The reason for this differentiated treatment was influenced by employment potential after students completed the program. At that time, kindergarten programs in which graduates could find work were supported by private institutions or located in philanthropic agencies. Such venues relied upon volunteers and paid modest salaries.

Kindergartners continued to promote the values of early education, sometimes paying rent to school systems for the privilege of conducting classes in a public school building. When school systems offered free kindergarten classes in a neighborhood school as a free public service, community pressure more often than not created a clamor for kindergarten continuation at taxpayer expense.

In 1924 Patty Smith Hill was hired to conduct a nursery school on the campus of Columbia University, and she invited a national group of professionals to a conference at the university. Those invited to meet and consider the current state of early-childhood services were at that time working in a variety of nationwide child-care programs that provided educational services for preschool children.

This meeting disseminated valuable information for organizing the field and produced a professional organization for dealing with discrepancies in services provided to help calm public confusion about the education and care of young children. In addition, this group formed the National Committee on Nursery Schools to supplant the variety of fringe affiliates.

By the 1930s, following the Great Depression, our nation's public policies were being designed to head off family destitution and hunger by providing employment primarily for men and male teens. A number of projects to benefit unemployed youth and their families were promoted under a federal initiative called the Civilian Conservation Corps. The program for adult males, and to lesser degree females, was called the Works Progress Administration.

There was a significant increase in federally financed public works projects like the construction of new schools, hospitals, post offices, highways, and bridges, all created to reduce the effects of a 25-percent unemployment rate during the Great Depression of the 1930s. This social policy initiative was labeled the New Deal.

Community interest created by the New Deal raised expectations among neighborhood advocates for child-care and settlement-house expansion. This helped to create advocates for an improvement in neighborhood schools through an inclusion of after-school programs and parent-community organizations.

Aimed at improving economic opportunities for families, these improvements often included vocational training like home economics, auto mechanics, carpentry crafts, and teaching opportunities in expanded kindergartens. For schools in large metropolitan areas like New York City, Chicago, and Los Angeles, this meant auditoriums, swimming pools, and sports stadiums, just to name a few.

These building initiatives occurred at about the same time that state universities integrated *normal schools* into higher education. What were formerly known as normal schools can best be described as equivalent to our present-day high school level of study.

As normal schools became a part of four-year colleges and universities, they selected *home economics* as the area of study for *kindergartners* (teachers of kindergarten children); later, departments of home economics became departments of Early Childhood Education and Development. Laboratory schools (training sites) and campus child-care centers emerged some time later to serve children of faculty and students while providing observational facilities for early childhood training and study, in support of academic experiences for early-childhood majors.

In addition to these gradual advances, the *National Committee on Nursery Schools* and its affiliates changed the organization's name and focus. Today it is known as the *National Association for the Education of Young Children*, and has expanded its membership. During the same period, the International Kindergarten Union, reduced its commitment to Froebel's nationally accepted early-childhood framework and became the *Association for Childhood Education International*.

Today, Early Childhood Education and Development is recognized by all professional teacher groups as a significant division of education. Education is a field of study but not a *discipline* in the same sense as geography, history, science, and mathematics are. Each area of academic study selects theories to support their informed *philosophy, theory,* and *practice*. And there are historical underpinnings for all studies that help to frame a professional practice. Teaching is an essential professional practice. Early Childhood Education and Development, in defining its practice, selects from a variety of theoretical fields, primarily anthropology and psychology.

On the list of individuals whose works continue to frame theory and practice trends in Early Childhood and Development are Erik Erikson, Sigmund

Freud, Maria Montessori, Jean Piaget, B. F. Skinner, and Lev Vygotsky. This book will discuss the intellectual framework of these theorists and others who helped shape classroom practices in Early Childhood Education and Development.

In the late 1800s and early 1900s studies of early-childhood growth and development attracted broad-based attention. This period displays the work of Sigmund Freud, and John Dewey, and works of Freud and Dewey are often discussed along with the theories of Jean Piaget and Erik Erikson. Piaget and Erikson appeared later in the 1900s. By this time, activists and teachers in the kindergarten movement in the United States were called *kindergartners,* and this term will be used throughout this text. Families that decide to school their children at home will be referred to in this text as *home schoolers.*

Childhood was an integral part of Sigmund Freud's *psychosexual* theories. Freud detailed childhood growth and development in steps and stages, noting behavioral expectations by age. Freud's knowledge and subsequent theories of childhood were acquired from his own memory and memories revealed to Freud by his patients during their therapy sessions.

Childhood was also basic to the philosophy of John Dewey. Dewey's philosophy described the essential nature of knowledge acquisition as enabling a learner's freedom of action and thought. Erik Erikson's theme followed the Freudian pathway but subdued Freud's emphasis on the impact of sexual difference and brought our attention to issues that are best described as *psychosocial* (Erikson, 1950).

Jean Piaget, a biologist and the youngest in this group, studied his own children through observations and discussions with them about their interpretations of their perceptions. He followed their flow of logical reasoning and compared their descriptions with those of other children.

His early knowledge of assessment in child development came, in part, from working on the task of scaling tests for children in the lab of Cyril Burt. This employment came at a time when his wife was expecting their first child. His theories have been reviewed and analyzed for some time now, and his work remains significant in the field of early childhood.

With specific reference to early-childhood education and development, there remains too little understanding of this discipline by education agencies because it does not fit comfortably into the K–12 education model. The scope of early-childhood education and development starts at birth and extends through age eight. K–12 education starts at kindergarten (approximately age five), and ends in grade 12 (approximately age 17). This places a burden on statewide public policy to maintain two pathways for early childhood–age children—one pathway is committed to early childhood *education,* and the other is committed to early childhood *care.* Early-childhood education is the responsibility of tax-supported public schools (K–3), while early childhood care (birth–2) is the responsibility of a confusing variety of state and federal social agencies.

Historically, researchers in the field of early childhood have published infant intelligence scales, along with tests for evaluating hearing and speech, personal-social skills, eye-hand performance, and intelligence, just to name a few. In this group we can identify Mary Ainsworth, Nancy Bayley, T. Berry Brazelton, Arnold Gesell, Ruth Griffiths, Jean Piaget, Sandra Scarr, Ina C. Uzgiris, J. McVicker Hunt, and David Wechsler. This book will discuss their work.

Finally, I am deeply concerned about the public view of teaching as a profession. Criticism is heard too frequently from various commissions, blue-ribbon study and focus groups, and media concerning the shortcomings of public schools and our teachers. When we are applauding the achievements of astronauts, neuroscientists, physicians, and the like, we tend to forget that at various times in the lives of these renowned people, they have been in kindergarten, fourth grade, junior high, high school, and the like. It is often the work of teachers who informed and inspired many notables who have brought great benefits to us all, after acquiring a foundation of knowledge that made them competent.

Historical Perspectives

Over the last two hundred years, teachers often have been unfairly criticized and even ridiculed. Their methods of instruction and selection of cur-
ricular materials have been challenged with their approaches to discipline
and even their preparation and effectiveness in the classroom have rou-
tinely been second-guessed by politicians, educational reformers, and the
public at large.

—David H. and Jo Ann Parkerson (2001)

This chapter provides a comprehensive review of a historical perspective of
early childhood, one that spans almost two hundred years. Perspectives are
examined through a review of contributions made by individuals to the field
of Early Childhood Education and Development. The selection of these individuals is guided by their contributions to significant segments of early childhood study.

Some of their contributions have added to our overall understanding of
how society viewed childhood during selected periods, while other contributions have focused on developmental issues related to birth, infancy, growth,
and development. All individuals were carefully selected because of the value
of their work to a study of early childhood as we know it today.

The ideas and works of John Comenius and John Locke are essential in significantly different ways. Both provided an appreciation of the history of
Early Childhood Education during the 1600s. John Comenius had a direct impact on how parents interacted with their children. John Locke influenced our
views concerning citizenship and individualism. He also provided convenient
justifications for European colonization in foreign lands. Such justifications,

when extended to lands in the United States, raise implications for the enslavement of African Americans, the destruction of Native American cultures, and the oppression of Hispanics.

Johann Frederich Oberlin, a visionary who was the first to organize schooling for children under the age of six, and Johann Pestalozzi, whose schools for young children were designed to head off their trip into poverty as their families before them, were the first to introduce free education for young children from poor families. They were true pioneers of education for infants and other young children, and their work was significant during the 1700s.

Robert Owen established schools in Europe and sometime later introduced a school in the United States for children as young as two years old. Owen's school was envisioned as central to a community-based idea designed to serve the needs of its residents.

During the 1800s, Margaret and Rachel McMillan were providing childcare for poor and homeless children in England while Margarethe Schurz and Elizabeth Peabody were establishing kindergartens in the United States with curricula developed by Friedrich Froebel, a pioneer in kindergarten education in Germany. In the early 1900s, the world was awakened to the educational theories of Maria Montessori, a medical doctor in Italy. Her ideas led the way for advanced views that children need not be tracked based upon academic performance, but the education of all children, working independently in the same classroom with appropriate materials, was possible.

During the later 1900s, important theoretical influences were drawn into the field of early childhood from the psychology of Sigmund Freud, John Dewey, Lev Vygotsky, Jean Piaget, and Erik Erikson. In addition to these major figures, there are those who contributed to the history of early childhood in indirect ways, and these contributors will be noted throughout these historical discussions in their appropriate places.

Persons mentioned have influenced theory and practice for early childhood growth and development, and provided important information for teachers and parents. They all became well known for their ideas.

These important figures are all cited for advancing ideas about child development, and they did so with a dedication to all ages of humanity. An examination of their achievements during their lifetime reveals their contributions to advancements in various categories. Johann Pestalozzi, for his time, was an expert on the theory and practice of modern farming and worked to pass these skills on to poor families in Zurich primarily through teaching their children.

Friedrich Froebel studied science, mathematics, and languages at the University of Gottingen and worked as a museum mineralogist for a time in Berlin. John Comenius was a theologian and member of the United Brethren

Clergy. Robert Owen had several careers. He was an entrepreneur, industrialist, a pioneer of the British labor movement, and a social visionary. In *The Marriage System of the New Moral World,* a book that he published in 1813, Owen supported equality for women, including their access to divorce and other rights. As one biographer described his life: "Owen lived not so much a long life as a sequence of historical episodes." (Cole, 1953)

John Comenius, a Moravian minister during the 1600s, is noted for his revolutionary ideas about the cooperative child-rearing relationships between mothers, fathers, and their infants. During a period when fathers seldom interacted with their young children, Comenius emphasized that childhood teaching and learning should be a sharing relationship between parents.

Johann Pestalozzi, working primarily in Switzerland, gained recognition for his work with young children under the age of six. At one time in his work he hired Friedrich Froebel early in Froebel's career to assist in this work.

Friedrich Froebel became well known because of his influence among pioneers of the kindergarten movement in Germany and the United States. He influenced and trained early-childhood professionals in the United States who traveled to Germany in the late 1800s and early 1900s to observe his work and study with him. Historical foundations of studies in early childhood can be traced to the kindergarten movement.

With the exception of the United States, where the influence of Froebel was created primarily by his advocates and students, the kindergarten movement had a modest influence outside of Germany. This lack of support for kindergartens in Europe was not helped by a prohibition against kindergartens enacted in Prussia in 1851.

By 1910, the world of parents and teachers was excited by news of the Montessori Educational System, a system of schooling that included in the same classrooms naturally competent learners alongside learners who, for a variety of reasons, might have been reluctant learners because of intellectual and/or physical limitations. In Montessori's view, academic work is not exhausting but naturally exhilarating for children.

It is difficult to identify a precise starting point for a study of infants and toddlers as an area of Early Childhood Education and Development. To many, a specific starting point for rising interests in infant and toddler issues is not significant because for them, events in the lifetime of the early-childhood profession are more important than a historical entry point in time; for those, we have several observations.

Most historians identify Johann F. Oberlin as the first to single out infants as a group in his education centers, and notations are cited in the Oberlin section of this chapter. On the other hand, Sadie Ginsberg, an established leader in childcare and the executive director of the Child Study Association of

Maryland, gives Robert Owen credit for establishing the first childcare center in the United States.

> Exact beginnings are always hard to pinpoint but most authorities give credit to the Scottish mill owner and social reformer—Robert Owen—for establishing what we would think of as a childcare center: a place for the children of working mothers with some idea of a program, consciously staffed with the needs of children in mind. . . . Robert Owen was an idealist sincerely troubled by the suffering people. Himself a mill owner, he firmly believed that industrialists had a responsibility to do something for the children of workers. (Hymes, 1978–1979, p. 7)

Oberlin and Owen will be discussed later in this section as their life span is appropriately placed chronologically within the framework of other pioneers in early childhood.

JAN AMOS COMENIUS (JAN AMOS KOMENSKY) (1592–1670)

Comenius is often credited with being among a small group of original thinkers who framed the ideas that led to modern educational theory. Comenius and his family were members of the Czech Reformist Church, commonly known as the Unity of Brethren.

Born in Nivince, Moravia, on March 28, 1592, Comenius pursued equal access to education for girls and boys while stressing a significant role for both parents in the education of their children. His ideas for early education suggested that it should start at birth with mothers and fathers taking turns in the role of "teacher." These recommendations came during a period when affluent families hired others (sometimes called wet nurse, servant, and maid) to raise their children.

Comenius was opposed to the common practice of women caring for babies in one group, and men relieved of child-caring tasks in the other. This made Comenius the earliest proponent of the equal rights for women.

After completing grade school, Comenius attended a school run by Unitas Fratrum (United Brethren), a Protestant school at Perov. The Brethren supported an equal opportunity for religious education for men and women, probably the source of Comenius's liberal perspectives.

After graduation, Comenius traveled to Germany for advanced studies in theology. While studying in Germany, he married and had two children. During this time he studied with Calvinist scholars like David Pareus, Joann Fisher, and Joann Alstead (Comenius, 1901).

With a family to support, Comenius accepted a teaching job. During this time he became an ordained minister and head of the church school at Fulnek.

He authored an important book for his time, titled *School of Infancy*. It was in this text that he talked directly to parents concerning their roles in the education of their young. "When we lift them up, put them to rest, show them anything, or smile on them, we aim that they in turn should look on us, smile, reach out their hands to take what we give" (Comenius, 1957, p. 98).

After the completion of studies at the University of Heidelberg and the University of Herborn, Comenius was an ordained minister, and was later promoted to a bishop in a reform church. While still in Czechoslovakia, Comenius started work on an encyclopedia of universal knowledge. An anti-Hapsburg uprising in his country interrupted this project and led to the loss of independence in the geographic area where Comenius and his family resided.

During the following years, his country's expansion of Catholicism forced Comenius into hiding. It was during this time in isolation that he wrote *The Labyrinth of the World and the Paradise of the Heart*. This book became one of his best-known works, but Comenius never returned to his country. He finally settled in Leszno, Poland.

As early as the eighteenth century, influenced in part by opportunities for higher education, the most learned people in society were the clergy. It was also common during that period that only boys were educated, with the primary objective being preparation for the clergy (Murphy, 1996; Aries, 1962). Therefore, during university-level education, it was unlikely that men and women would be students together.

During his adult career, Comenius encouraged universal-educational initiatives, regardless of sex, and these ideas were radical for his time. Such ideas were extreme for that period, because institutions of higher learning and elevated positions of clergy leadership were only available to men (Sadler, 1966).

The most significant innovation in his book for children was the divided page. In this regard, a line down the center of each page divided the English text from the Latin. This enabled readers of either language to increase their knowledge of the language with which they had fewer skills. Another innovation appeared in a book for children titled *The Visible World* (1659), which included illustrations appearing on the same page as its matching text. Children in the prereading stage often "read" a story that they have heard many times by looking at the pictures. It is remarkable that Comenius, during this early period, had developed an awareness of this childhood strategy.

Today, an area of emphasis for early-childhood practitioners is language acquisition. Some theorists suggest that a child's knowledge of language is acquired primarily through imitation and memory. Others, like Vygotsky, for example, suggest that children quickly learn language through social interactions by finding out what works and what does not (1986). Comenius suggested that when these "mature adults" are known by children as their parents, the potential for learning is improved significantly (1901).

He also recommended that child/parent activities involve mothers and fathers alternating in sharing reading activities with their children. These ideas were advanced by Comenius during a time when fathers avoided interactions with their infants until they were walking and talking. Comenius's recommendations to parents were remarkable for the 1600s. Parents of the 1600s had to deal with a social environment that valued children in terms of how their labor could be sold to satisfy the needs of their family. It was common for children as young as six years of age to be hired out by their parents. In the late 1800s, it was the work of Maria Montessori that was destined to change the lives of these children.

During the time of Comenius, children who were unable to work for physical or mental challenges were at times cast out by families, and such children survived through their cunning or success as beggars. Such circumstances were so prevalent that novelists like Charles Dickens penned stories like *Oliver Twist* and *A Christmas Carol,* detailing the tragedy of poor families and children living on the streets of London.

Robert Owen in the late 1700s petitioned the British legislature to make changes to accommodate the safety and security of abandoned children. Margaret McMillan and Rachael McMillan almost 100 years later identified similar problems in London. This led to the McMillan sisters' establishing a residential home for homeless and abandoned children in London. Their center included baths, clean clothing, recreational play, and schooling. This served as the model for Maria Montessori's children's center, *Casa dei Bambini,* in Italy in the late 1800s.

To many students of the period, Comenius was a political activist. He went to Berlin to convene with Czech exiles, meeting with many other notables, like philosopher and mathematician Descartes. Because his religious affiliations and beliefs were out of favor in the geographic areas where he lived, it was ironic that, often during his absence, tragedy befell his wife and children (Murphy, 1996).

Influenced by philosopher, essayist, and statesman Francis Bacon (1561–1626), Comenius' contributions to what is known as early childhood education theory today can be observed in the works and influences of Jean Piaget, Maria Montessori, Eurie Bronfenbrenner, Erik Erikson, Sigmund Freud, and John Dewey. Comenius as a philosopher proposed that the learned of the world pursue a fluid and dynamic universal knowledge base that could blend a practical human knowledge shared by all regardless of gender, religion, language, or racial origin.

In general, Comenius believed that the work of the school and church, along with other universal institutions, should strive for a social synthesis where all ideas, modern and ancient, could be brought into a common understanding and acceptance. The Comenius connection to the thought of Freud, Erikson, and Piaget can be understood through his ideas of human development, where practical human activity is viewed as pointing the way toward lifelong dynamic universal reforms.

JOHN LOCKE (1632–1704)

At the beginning of each school year, teachers will collect official forms from parents as proof that their school-age children have been inoculated against certain childhood diseases that at one time in our history were prevalent. This prevention procedure is done to protect *all* children from the contagious effects of certain infections common in schools.

Each time this procedure is carried out, however, a relatively small number of children will become ill. The notion that it is acceptable for a relatively small number of children to suffer the discomforts of low-level infections for the benefit of most children who remain relatively free of infections emerged from the advocacy of John Locke.

Locke proposed that a policy benefiting the majority of citizens, while producing minor discomforts for a few citizens, was a policy trade-off worthy of enforcement. The framers of the Constitution were readers of Locke's philosophical writings and influenced by his ideas. Locke thought that individuals required a strong, comprehensive set of laws to protect citizens from each other. His philosophy suggested that individuals are naturally self-serving. He believed that without an extensive set of laws and their rigorous enforcement, few people would be safe. It is this line of thought that eventually led to Rousseau's rejection of Locke's philosophy.

In Rousseau's popularized philosophy, the public already had too many laws controlling their behavior. In his view, most laws were designed to expand the rights of wealthy landowners and the well-connected, leaving the less-affluent with too few rights to pursue their interests in privacy.

Among the first self-assigned tasks of our John Locke–influenced post–Revolutionary War government was for colonies in United States to create and establish a constitution. Governing bodies in some of the colonies had already tried their hand at developing a "constitution" to govern their communities. These documents, prepared in colonies, existed in various stages prior to the writing of our present-day national constitution.

Somewhat later, for our country's final document, James Madison and other writers of our national constitution borrowed several ideas and some of the language from documents originating in the colonies, and these writings became a part of our country's final document. Native Americans, African Americans, and poor whites who were not owners of property were granted few rights, or in the case of slaves, they were viewed as property.

This philosophy was commonly accepted during Locke's time and satisfied governments, wealthy families, and the church. Locke's philosophy suggested that the primary purpose of government was to create and enforce laws to protect citizens from each other. The ideas that individuals are born in sin and naturally evil from birth were teachings of the church and embedded in Locke's philosophy. This philosophy went on to suggest that if desires of the masses were left unchecked, the implications of this original sin could be acted out. Infringements on the rights of individuals by the church or the king were not thought important during these times.

The Spanish and English had been on the American continent for some time, and parts of the continent had been annexed by the British. After the Revolutionary War, many British remained and were joined by other Europeans. Some came as planters seeking benefit from relatively free labor from indentured whites and enslaved blacks. They were especially pleased through Locke's philosophy that they had the support of God and religion for land acquisitions. Additionally, their self-serving pursuits were often perceived as benevolent "God's work."

Locke's writings suggested that God looked with disfavor upon caretakers of the land who allowed that land to lie fallow without growing products for consumption or profit. This philosophy opened the way for the British and other white planters to acquire the land of Native Americans for the growth and production of cotton and tobacco to appear godly.

Despite the fact that many of our early leaders who wrestled our country from Native Americans learned from Locke, John Locke was not a teacher in the true sense of the word; he was a philosopher. He wrote extensively, usually in support of organized government, landowners, and his wealthy friends.

It should not be surprising then, that early schooling in the United States reflected John Locke's philosophy. Early classrooms were firmly structured, strictly controlled, and teacher centered. Needs of society were more important than needs of the learner. As Locke wrote, the needs of individuals should be subsumed within the needs of society (Locke, 1968). Even today, a common criticism directed at public school graduates comes from industries seeking low-cost labor. It is their view that public schools should supplant their job training, and graduates should be able to start work without the requirement that employers bear this cost.

Individuals whose work was influenced by Locke and whose theories were adopted by educators in the 1950s and 1960s include James Watson and B. F. Skinner, two psychologists whose theories practically captured classroom education of the 1950s and 1960s (Watson, 1928; Skinner, 1957). Today, theories of Watson and Skinner can be found in many behavior-modification approaches described in books on classroom-management principles.

The Lancaster system, first introduced in England, was later implemented in large public schools in the United States. It was a perfect fit for teacher-centered methods that were common in our country's public schools at that time. The Lancaster system was a method of organizing and controlling student movement in schools. The system also assured student conformity to school rules through an extensive use of students as partial teachers and administrative monitors (Lancaster, 1821). The Lancaster system made it possible for a single adult to administer a school of 600 children. By the 1930s, John Dewey, an advocate for child-centered education, gained considerable notice from the teaching profession, a profession that was ready for a system of education that invited students to participate in their own learning. By this time, most schools had abandoned the Lancaster system.

The work of John Dewey eventually gave rise to a variety of student-centered teaching initiatives, including *progressive education, cooperative education, the open classroom, affective education,* and *humanistic education.*

By the mid-1960s, public policy initiated the *Elementary and Secondary Education Act* (1965), *Project Head Start* (1965), *Project Follow Through,* (1967), the *Child Abuse Prevention Act,* (1973), the *Education for all Handicapped Children Act* (1977), the *Gifted and Talented Act* (1978), and the *Federal Preschool and Early Intervention Act* (1986).

JEAN-JACQUES ROUSSEAU (1712–1778)

Rousseau is often discussed in the same context with John Locke. This is done because some descriptions of their philosophies can be seen in a context of opposition.

Philosophers, theorists, and practitioners on whose work Rousseau's philosophy was influential include Johann Pestalozzi, Robert Owen, Johann Oberlin, Friedrich Froebel, John Dewey, Lev Vygotsky, Jean Piaget, Erik Erikson, and J. McVicker Hunt.

Rousseau was born eight years after the death of John Locke. He, therefore, had a more modern society within which to interact with thinkers during our most recent past. This "modern" society continued many of the fundamentals reflected in the philosophy of Locke. Rousseau's ideas about the education were advanced for his time, and reflected theories that had been first introduced over 100 years earlier by John Comenius.

Rousseau's philosophy concerning the education of children can be extrapolated from his novel *Emile*. It is probably available in some form in many libraries today (1964, 1762). In this novel, the relationship between a tutor and his pupil is used as a framework for describing what Rousseau considers the ideal relationship between a teacher and learner (Boyd, 1911).

In Rousseau's view, adults of his time knew very little about how children learn. The most efficient manner through which teachers could find out how children learn, according to Rousseau, was to allow a relationship between the teacher and learner to emerge that encouraged the learner to freely *interact* with the teacher in an atmosphere of trust and cooperation. This *interaction* would motivate teachers and learners to be inquisitive, actively questioning, and eager to add new information derived from teacher-learner interactions (Green, 1955).

A view that is consistent throughout *Emile* is the teacher-learner relationships that encourage (or allow) learner freedom. Teachers who are more successful at enabling knowledge acquisition for young children are better able to provide productive foundations for children to achieve intellectual resolve when they are faced with problems on their own.

> We know nothing about childhood; and with our mistaken notions the further we advance the more we go astray. The wisest writers devote themselves to what a man ought to know, without asking what a child is capable of learning. (Rousseau, 1979, p. 1)

The encouragement of learner freedom in a manner in which information gathered from children is essential to planning for their future learning needs found its way into Friedrich Froebel's kindergarten movement in Germany, and ultimately became a significant part of nursery school, preschool, and kindergarten curriculum in the United States (Froebel, 1900).

Rousseau's theories about how children learn have experienced different treatments and different levels of valuing by educators. In the 1960s, Rousseau's philosophy was highly valued in the United States because of a prevalence of humanistic public opinion. It was a period when public opinions favored antiracist public policy, opportunities for student participation in higher education policy matters and the planning of their own academic path were increased, and antiwar demonstrations were prevalent, and there emerged a relaxation of adult controls over the lives of young adults. By 1920, the *Jean-Jacques Rousseau Institute* was reorganized as a part of Geneva University, and Jean Piaget was appointed its codirector (Ginsburg and Opper, 1969).

JOHANN FREDERIC OBERLIN (1740–1826)

In 1767 Jean F. Oberlin established, at his own expense, the first school for children under the age of six, in a rural coal-mining community in the French countryside. Oberlin established several schools for families of the working poor. He recruited teachers for this new and innovative enterprise, and named them *conductices.*

With schools for children being introduced in different parts of the world, it is not unusual that questions concerning the *first* educator to accomplish this task for *infants* would arise. A part of this problem arises when the definition of *infancy* is examined. The first six months of life are mostly defined as the *neonatal* period. Infancy is defined by some (including the author) as the developmental period from birth to 12 months; yet others have defined the period of infancy to extend from birth to 24 months. It is this latter designation that classifies infancy to the age of two years; therefore, schools for two-year-olds can be classified as *infant schools.*

Rusk (1967) has suggested that schools that integrate infants with older children should not be classified as infant schools. With this variable in mind, one would classify schools founded by Johann Frederic Oberlin and Robert Owen as infant schools, but not those founded by others where infants are integrated throughout classes for older children. For example, those founded by Pestalozzi and de Fellenberg should not be labeled infant schools.

> Claims have been advanced that various educators other than Oberlin founded the infant school, for example Pestalozzi and de Fellenberg, but these must be rejected. Although we have seen, Pestalozzi, by the introduction of his *Anschauungsunterricht,* made possible an education specially suited to infants, in practice he made no attempt to segregate the youngest pupils and educate them separately. (Rusk, 1967, p. 107)

Oberlin's first teachers came from a group of local women from whose ranks wealthy families hired tutors for their children to prepare them for a successful integrated life in affluent Paris society. Oberlin interviewed, hired, and trained his new teachers to conduct classes by sitting with their group of children, encouraging language interaction and storytelling as starting points for art and music, along with learner-initiated project-construction activities. During these teacher-child interactions, which included teachers telling stories and conversations with individuals and the group, the conductices simultaneously worked on their knitting. Because of this casual, interactive style of teaching, Oberlin's schools were sometimes called "knitting schools."

The establishment of learning environments where the teacher joined students in conversation to encourage their participation in the planning for the day is prominent in today's early childhood classrooms; this style is sometimes called "rug meetings." It is a type of procedure that, in the early 1900s, was often negatively valued by Maria Montessori.

The Maria Montessori model required that individual work assignments given to learners must be designed for use by each learner following one-on-one teacher explanation and direction. In this regard, predesigned Montessori materials would be required, and the Montessori "directress" would explain and direct the use of the learning material(s) by individual students (Kramer, 1976).

In the Oberlin model, the conductice, through the teacher's observation during group interactions, becomes aware of each student's needs, strengths, and weaknesses, enabling future interactions to become teaching opportunities. Here, the knowledge and skills that are revealed from observations of each learner, or appear common to the group, become staging points for future teaching objectives.

Montessori's rejection of Oberlin's and Froebel's group-interaction approaches was supplanted by Montessori teachers, who were trained to be aware of student competencies in advance, like age, economic status, knowledge, and skills acquired by the learner from previous Montessori classroom assignments, etc.

Because children in Oberlin's schools would probably spend their lives in a French working village or a modest vocation in Paris, they would be judged by their dialect. To know and use the dialect that was common to their poor coal-mining village would inhibit their access to opportunities outside of their present small-town environment. Therefore, Oberlin's educational objectives for his student included the acquisition of standard French that would be accepted in Paris society. Encouraging group and individual conversations with the conductices would be a major step toward achieving this goal. In a major part of his work, Oberlin emphasized language acquisition and use. In this regard, he published children's books and introduced many innovative ideas related to language.

JOHANN HEINRICH PESTALOZZI (1746–1827)

Pestalozzi brought the attention of families to the idea that children under the age of six could benefit more from teaching that was especially designed for their age group than from using the same practices for this age group as were used for children over the age of six. Pestalozzi's theories and practices became so well known that he frequently advised foreign government officials on schooling and curriculum matters, as well as educators worldwide who were designing curriculum materials for children under six.

His early work was directing services for young children in an orphanage in Stans, Switzerland. Here, he promoted the idea that caretaking adults could best serve the knowledge acquisition of young children by providing learning opportunities within a free and accessible environment that enabled learners to interpret meanings through their own observations (Green, 1913). Today, many early-childhood models are based on Pestalozzi's idea that, for children under six, learning should be suitable for the child's act of *making meaning.* This idea is also threaded through the work of Jean Piaget (1952).

For Pestalozzi, knowledge builds from the child's observations of human interactions and social circumstances where the behavior of others is available for the child's interpretations and can serve as a model for their own behavior. Years later, this idea can be found in the theories of Lev Vygotsky, the Russian psychologist.

Controlling the learner's experience (essential in the Montessori approach), according to Pestalozzi, inhibits the child's opportunity to freely experience, interact, and acquire the values inherent in individuality. As he worked with children in natural environments, like groups of children living on a farm with assigned chores, Pestalozzi refined the practices that emerged from his overall human philosophy.

To promote this gradually emerging practice from his philosophy, around 1800, he converted his farm into a school for poor children and introduced his practices about how children learn. Approximately twenty-five years later, he opened schools in Bergdorf and Yverden (Green, 1969). His ideas also fostered the founding of the London Infant School Society (later the Home and Colonial School Society). This group promoted the hiring of 150 Pestalozzi-trained teachers to educate newly hired teachers in 150 schools newly opened in England. Pestalozzi's work inspired the attachment of the title of "Pioneer of Modern Education" to an already long list of notable achievements (Silber, 1960).

As with many reformers, Pestalozzi's early life provides a gateway to understanding his lifelong commitment to social justice, especially for children. His father died when he was five, and all of his childhood benefits can be credited to his mother. He did not fare well in school and was thought to be physically vulnerable; often called "mother's boy," and "weakling," during a childhood period when he was a target of classmate jokes, this in part affected his academic work to the extent that his poor performance displeased his teachers. Pestalozzi's lack of success in school as a child, due to a moribund system of public education, helped shape his drive to improve on systems of educating young children by making them more learner sensitive (Pestalozzi, 1885).

He acquired considerable knowledge about his countrymen from traveling with his grandfather, a clergyman in Zurich. Needs of the peasant classes in

Switzerland became clear to Pestalozzi on these travels around the country-side. His first thought was that the knowledge of reading and writing would be of little help in providing a better life for children of the poor or their families. He recognized that many children of the poor spent their youth working long hours in factories for incomes that could hardly satisfy basic human needs. Travels with his grandfather to visit poor families are thought to have provided Pestalozzi with an inspiration to publish his story, *Leonard and Gertrude: Gertrude's Home School.*

> The holiday visits to his grandfather in his boyhood and his last eleven years at Neuhof brought him into intimate contact with the poor. He had himself suffered poverty, and as Pestalozzi said, only those who have themselves been poor really know how the poor live. These experiences were the source of the story, *Leonard and Gertrude*, which was published in 1783, 1785, and 1781. . . .
>
> Pestalozzi knew the village life of his native country as few of his contemporaries knew it, and in the first part of *Leonard and Gertrude* he is concerned especially with showing exactly the condition of affairs. In this simple story he makes clear the far reaching effects of a corrupt officialdom. Every household in the small community of Bonal suffers from the malicious influence of the man who at once is the village inn keeper and the official representative of the landowner. The whole atmosphere is contaminated, and the people are for the most part sunk in degraded and depraved poverty. There is, however, one exception, the household of his heroine, Gertrude, who is the model wife and mother. (Green, 1913, p. 29)

Pestalozzi's own experiences, very much like those about which he wrote, are thought to have influenced his overall philosophy that family life is a critical element in education, and that mothers are also a critical element. The intrinsic value of motherhood as a contributor to positive educational outcomes for children became the centerpiece of ideas framed by Comenius in the 1600s and were restated by Maria Montessori more than 100 years later.

ROBERT OWEN (1771–1858)

Robert Owen was truly a Renaissance man. In the early 1800s even with a limited capacity for the transmission of information, people worldwide had gained considerable knowledge of Pestalozzi's theories. Robert Owen was among the many who had read about him, and was significantly influenced by his ideas. This influence would have important implications years later for the United States.

Owen owned and supervised a weaving mill that employed as many 100 children at any given time. In the evening, he turned the manufacturing center into a Pestalozzi-style educational center that, among other things, turned the factory into a social center where educational opportunities were offered free to the daytime workers. Owen also established a school for children under six in Lanark, Scotland.

This creative display of Pestalozzi's ideas brought visitors from around the world and made Owen well known among the working classes. At the same time, consistent pressure was exerted on Owen by fellow manufacturers, who viewed his philanthropic activities as wasteful of profits. Owen eventually arrived in the United States where he planned to establish an entire community based on Pestalozzi-style cooperative community living with essential services like educational opportunities for families and children, starting at two years of age.

Born in Newton, Montgomeryshire, North Wales, in 1771, Owen had childhood experiences that tell the story of what bonded his lifelong interest to early childhood schooling. He was enrolled in school at the age of four. As in most parts of the English-speaking world, it was a mark of achievement if one had acquired the basic skills of reading and writing well enough for other readers to understand the writing. Owen had also learned to perform tasks that could engage the first four rules of arithmetic. Achievement of these skills gave Owen competency equal to that of his teacher (Cole, 1950).

After completion of the seventh grade, Owen was recognized by his teacher as the logical person to be his assistant. When Owen's father was approached by the teacher with this request, he was pleased to allow his son to serve in this capacity because it was a complimentary gesture, and it provided free tuition.

The idea of schools for infants was introduced in the United States early in the 1800s through the work of Owen. Owen had been a wealthy Welshman and supervisor, and later owner of a cotton mill where child laborers were employed along with adults. During a time when children as factory workers were treated as adult workers, Owen's benevolence as a social reformer provided educational opportunities after hours for workers. He was not comfortable with the common practice of children spending their days in factories, when in his view, all children should be in school like children of the affluent. This was also a time when it was highly profitable to own a cotton mill.

Because of what were considered unwarranted worker benefits by other cotton mill owners, Owen's industrialist colleagues exerted pressure against him. Weary of this opposition from other industrialists, Owen promptly left for the United States. Here he founded a cooperative self-sufficient community in Indiana, where, among other things, he introduced the idea of *infant schools*.

Robert Owen attracted a number of Pestalozzi-influenced professionals and scholars to his newly founded community of New Harmony, Indiana, along the Wabash River. Arriving by boat, this group included geologists, architects, Pestalozzi-trained teachers, chemists, and explorers. Their journey from Pennsylvania was termed a "boatload of scholars." Owen and his pioneers constructed several buildings thought essential for the convenience of town-folk, and they included a school.

In schools he had previously established in Scotland for the benefit of families working in his factory, Owen had forbidden corporal punishment and the coercion of pupils through threats. He advanced these principles in his work as a social reformer. In this regard Owen was aggressive in reducing the exploitation of children by leading drives in the British Parliament to regulate child labor. At that time, children as young as five working in cotton, wool, and flax mills, for example, were required to work unregulated for as long as mill owners demanded. It was not unusual, then, that Owen would continue to oppose such policies in the United States.

In the 1800s, similar exploitations of children in mill and factory work were widespread in the United States. Social reformers for the rights of children were actively involved in child labor reforms designed to reduce these oppressive conditions. In this group were Jane Addams, Lillian Wald, Jacob Riis, and other founders of the settlement-house and kindergarten movements. This aspect of child labor reform will be discussed later in this text.

Once in the United States, Owen sought a proper site for an ideal community where people could live a free and virtuous life. It was rather commonly known that several such communities already existed in the United States, and some were mentioned to Owen following his query.

The most well-known self-contained communities were those built by the Quakers in the northeast. In Philadelphia, for example, the Quakers were known for their persistent antislavery commitment to the extent that they had established schools for freed slaves, the most famous of which were the *African Free School* in New York and the *School for Colored Youth* in Philadelphia. The latter is known today as *Cheyney University*, and is the oldest predominantly African American university in the United States.

Owen settled on the purchase of a location in New Harmony, Indiana, that was previously owned by a religious group known as the Rappites. The success of the Rappites had been too modest for them to remain with their congregation, and they were pleased to sell their rights to Owen.

There was great enthusiasm in New York and Philadelphia for Owen's ideas, and several well-known professionals joined the community of New Harmony. Communities of this type were welcomed in the early 1800s by a relatively young United States, along with residential ideas of other social reformers, many similar in social structure. Owen and others with creative community-development ideas were aided by city planning departments for the purpose of expanding residential areas. The most prominent, and the organization from which Owen received assistance, was the New York Society for Promoting Communities.

New Harmony was an attempt by Owen to demonstrate that, starting with a foundation of early education for the young, communities could be organized into ideal socially cooperative environments. Robert Owen had published these ideas in *A New View of Society*, which appeared for sale before his arrival in New Harmony, in 1816.

It has been noted that the legacy of Robert Owen's New Harmony community rests on the imagination of some of its original residents. The most frequently mentioned are William McClure and Richard Flower. McClure, a Scots scientist, completed a geological survey of the United States and founded the Philadelphia Academy of Science. Richard Flower, along with McClure, laid the groundwork for a model of research and publishing that survives in today's universities.

This writing, however, intends to focus on Robert Owen's influence in shaping early childhood education in the United States. His influences are many; major among them was the founding of a school, established as the first of its kind in 1824.

Robert Dale Owen, the oldest son of Robert Owen who became the first president of Purdue University, published this description of the school in New Harmony, Indiana:

The "New Institution" or school, which is open for instruction of the children and young people connected with the establishment, to the number of about 600, consists of about two stories. The upper story, which is furnished with a double range of windows, one above the other, all round, is divided into two apartments; one which is the principal school-room, fitted with desks and forms, on the Lancaster plan, having a free passage down the centre of the room, is about 90 feet long, 40 feet broad, and 20 feet high. It is surrounded, except at one end, where a pulpit stands, with galleries, which are convenient, when this room is used, as it frequently is, either as a lecture room or place of worship. The other apartment on the second floor, is of the same width and height as that just mentioned, but only 49 feet long. The walls are hung round with representations of the most striking zoological and mineralogical specimens; including quadrupeds, birds, fishes, reptiles, insects, shells, minerals, andc. At one end there is a gallery, adapted for the purpose of an orchestra, and at the other are hung very large representations of the two hemispheres; each separate country, as well as the various seas, islands, being differently coloured, but without any names attached to them. This room is used as a lecture and ball room, and it is here, that the dancing and singing lessons are daily given. It is likewise occasionally used as a reading room for some of the classes. The lower story is divided into three apartments, of nearly equal dimensions, 12 feet high, and supported by hollow iron pillars, serving at the same time, as conductors, in winter, for heated air, which issues through the floor of the upper story, and by which means the whole building may, with ease, be kept at any required temperature. It is in these apartments that the younger classes are taught reading, natural history, and geography. (Silver, 1969, pp. 149–150)

Among other remarkable developments, the school accommodated children ages two to five, from 7:30 a.m. to 9 a.m., half the regular attendance time. For the remainder of the morning they engaged in free play. Children ages 6 to 12 remained from 10 a.m.–12 noon, and 3 p.m. to 5 p.m., and an evening school for those usually working during the day (over 12 years of age). Evening school offered the same academic subjects for children and older youth from 10 to 20 years of age.

Students were provided uniforms of high-quality white cotton in the shape of a Roman tunic. For boys the tunic reached the knee; for girls it extended to the ankles. Infant classes and evening classes were free, but to avoid a comparison with schools of charity, a minimal amount was charged for evening students, called "Scholars."

Only with special permission were families allowed to enter their children into paid employment prior to age 12. This policy in New Harmony preceded child labor laws in the United States. Later in New Harmony, a lack of employment opportunities for adults became a matter of discontent for those with modest incomes. From time to time the town had too few resources to accommodate resident needs.

Because of conflicts between socialistic principles and capitalist necessities the community survived for a few years and was disbanded. There was also criticism that children were being schooled without religious teaching. To this was a reply that all religions were recognized and studied for the purpose of enabling students to make informed choices of a particular religion to embrace, or decide to reject (Silver, 1969).

FRIEDRICH WILHELM AUGUST FROEBEL (1782–1852)

Friedrich Froebel was in search of the human experience that could balance the relationship between the individual and nature. He called this the *inner* and *outer* worlds of individual existence. Here, his purpose was twofold; the first was a personal quest to satisfy the need for self-actualization. The second need was to establish a theory from which he could shape theory and practice for his kindergarten ideas (Kilpatrick, 1916).

Froebel was set on the pathway toward his first goal when through his early educational encounters he associated with learned men of his time. His first apprenticeship placed him in the company of an outdoorsman who assigned Froebel, as a teen, to a forestry apprenticeship, which among other things, enabled him to spend his days exploring the beauty of nature (Lilley, 1967).

Toward the second goal, Froebel developed a curriculum with supportive learning materials and designed a pedagogical environment for young children; he named it *kindergarten*. Froebel's garden for children was inspired by his philosophy that early education can be a joy and effective when well-trained kindergarten teachers are encouraged to think of young children as healthy flourishing plants. Like plants, children, in their quest for growth and development, required watering (nurturing) and care (health).

An understanding of Froebel's curricula can start with his ideas about the usefulness of children's games in advancing the child's pursuit of comprehending the outside world. Froebel viewed children's play as their access to understanding the "inner" and "outer" pathway toward development.

In Froebel's view, the *inner* understanding comes from the child's inner direction for her own play and what the choice of games can mean to the self-selecting child. The child's *outer* understanding emerges from the natural outer forces on the child's play, as when a child is running and feeling the wind on her face or the playing child compares the relationship between stationary objects and her running, skipping, and hopping.

There is also a perceptual role for objects in this developmental process. Froebel developed a series of *gifts* for children to use in the kindergarten classroom. The basic toy is a ball. Froebel thought that the ball was a basic design that reacts to its use in play in a fundamentally mathematical manner. Froebel's gifts (games), when placed in use by the developing child, represented movement in the *outer* world when acted upon by the child for her own purpose (joy, competition, boredom, etc.). The child's own purpose is Froebel's *inner* world (Froebel, 1900).

> He inspired a new understanding of children's activities and ways of learning, and directed attention to their need for manifold experiences if they are to arrive at awareness of themselves and their world. He strove to show the significance of the child's earliest years and of his relationship to mother and family. He saw that the young child needs a special environment in which to grow and learn and so he established the institution to which he gave the name kindergarten. (Lilley, 1967, p. 2)

Froebel's dedication to early schooling and child development was probably influenced by his own less than enjoyable childhood. After the death of his mother, his father, a strict Lutheran minister, remarried. His stepmother left Friedrich in the care of servants and for a time sent him to a school for girls. During his early teens he was under the supervision of his mother's brother, who sent him to a school for boys. Here he was unpopular because he could not keep pace with the rugged games that were commonly played.

Before his 16th birthday, about the time when boys were being considered for admission to a university, his parents decided to send him to apprentice with a forester. While in this role, it is believed, direct contact with nature for long hours, along with an early life that lacked a robust interaction with peers, helped him formulate his approach to life. A belief that all development is driven by one law was later introduced to Froebel while a student at the University of Göttingen through his relationship with his mineralogy professor (Lilley, 1967).

As was true for Maria Montessori, who entered the university as engineering major then quickly switched to medicine, Froebel entered the university to study architecture, a major that soon changed to education. Here, he found himself in a school whose director had been a student of Pestalozzi, who at the time was unknown to Froebel. While at the university in Frankfurt he taught a group of 35 teenage boys in a model school for two years. From observations of his work and an assessment of his style, he was advised by the school's director to observe at the Pestalozzi Institute at Yverdon. His work with Pestalozzi was inspiring because in many ways Pestalozzi's ideas were in confluence with his own.

Froebel received a commission to tutor three brothers and took them with him to Pestalozzi's school in Yverdon. Impressed with young Friedrich, Pestalozzi encouraged him to expand his activities with the boys to include play and nature study.

Froebel's ideas concerning child growth and development were also influenced by his readings of other philosophers, like John Comenius and Jean-Jacques Rousseau. His search also led him to the works of Johann Gottlieb Fichte, Immanuel Kant, and Georg Wilhelm Friederich Hegel (Lawrence, 1969).

Born in Thuringia, Germany, following his experience of working with Pestalozzi, Froebel opened his school for children the small German village of Blankenberg. His first use of the name *kindergarten* was in 1829.

Friedrich's lack of mobility usually found in young boys of this period was thought to be caused by home confinement, reducing his opportunities to actively play with others in his age group. An uncle, during conversations with young Friedrich, viewed his homebound restrictions as inhibiting his development, and asked his brother (Friedrich's father), permission to care for his nephew as a resident in his home (Shapiro, 1983).

Friedrich's father agreed with his brother that his son's opportunity to run and romp, under supervision, around the grounds of his home would be beneficial for his health and well-being. Friedrich recognized the differences between the two environments. One restricted his experiences by confining them to the indoors, and the other environment allowed great freedom to experience an almost unlimited variety of the out-of-doors. Experiences with living, growing, and natural environments are thought to have awakened Friedrich's lifelong interests in the relationship between humans and other living things (Kilpatrick, 1916).

Froebel's attempts to put his ideas into writing can be found in letters, pamphlets, and articles intended to describe his ideas about early education. The most famous writing can be found in his major work, *The Education of Man* (1887). This has been described as a commendable description of his early ideas, accompanied by a strong consistent continuity of thought. Despite this major work, Froebel's cumbersome writing style has not attracted the number of readers to study his works that one would expect (Lilley, 1967).

> His style is verbose, repetitive, convoluted. There are long rhetorical passages, peculiar word-plays and eccentric emphases. He would never listen to criticism or use the accepted philosophical terms. However, it is in *The Education of Man* that the main clues to Froebel's thought lie. The book contains both the ideas which he formed early in his career and the germinal points of his later discoveries in the field of young children's education. (Lilley, 1967, p. 4)

The freedom of learners to engage their environment was basic to Froebel's theory. Froebel's curriculum was designed to provide a physical framework within which young children and their Froebel-trained teachers could enable young learners to understand their inner and outer worlds. When one considers the view of childhood held by general society, it is easier to understand the world for which Froebel curricula were being prepared (Liebschner, 2001).

Children from poor families were put to work in income-producing enterprises as young as seven years old. Children worked in manufacturing on heavy dangerous machinery in poorly ventilated areas, sometimes in the dark, for twelve hours a day. This was not considered cruel by most people of that time. Now imagine that during this time of institutionalized child cruelty, educators suggest that children should be in school and not in factories. Attitudes that shaped Pestalozzi's and Froebel's time also shaped the ways in which they had to frame their ideas about poor children to fit those times.

In the early 1900s in cities like Chicago, New York, and Philadelphia, in neighborhoods that were overpopulated with Black migrants and European immigrants, social-service agencies opened settlement houses (sometimes called community centers). Froebel-inspired kindergartens, Dalcroze dance and music groups, second-language classes, and instructional seminars on voting and applying for jobs were included among a variety of other services.

Their most significant service provided to these neighborhoods was a Froebel kindergarten. When not teaching, kindergartners made home visits to educate younger children at home and inform parents about additional social services in their city. Froebel's curriculum for kindergarten was developed for a period when children in poor German families were held in the same low regard as were immigrant children in the early 1900s. By the 1940s, settlement-house social workers joined social activists in support of social policy that, among other things, led to the enactment of women's rights, anti-lynching legislation, and legislation that eliminated cruel child-labor practices (Addams, 1910, 1964).

ELIZABETH PEABODY (1804–1894)

Born in Billerica, Massachusetts, Elizabeth Palmer Peabody can be credited with the advancement of English-language kindergartens in the United States. She grew up in a home-schooling environment that was rich with intellectual inquirers. Her self-taught mother, who had little formal education, conducted a school for young women, and a young Elizabeth was one of the teachers in her mother's school.

When the Peabody family moved to Lancaster, Massachusetts, Elizabeth, being the oldest child in the family, took charge of her mother's school. Growing up in a family whose parents were influenced by the Unitarian religion, Elizabeth developed a worldview that considered slavery as an act of evil and the U.S. policy regarding Native Americans as cruel. Her interest in the concept of kindergartens, after an introduction to the idea by Margarethe Schurz, a Froebel student, motivated her to read the writings of Froebel, and ultimately seek his face-to-face guidance.

During Peabody's adult life, her hometown of Boston was an active area for academic explorations. Many notable writers and educators traveled in the company of Peabody and her sisters. This group, often identified as *transcendentalists,* included Henry Bernard, William Ellery Channing, Margaret Fuller, Horace Mann, Amos Bronson Alcott, Ralph Waldo Emerson, Nathaniel Hawthorne, and Henry David Thoreau.

For her time, Peabody was among a few women academically knowledgeable enough to hold her own among the most educated men of her time. She wrote books and articles and translated Greek, German, Italian, and Latin into English. She also participated in discussion groups and book clubs in the homes of other learned women, and was a prodigious writer, enjoying taking notes and recording events.

Peabody's knowledge of *transcendentalism* was inspired by learned men and women of Massachusetts. Being well read, she derived gratification from interacting with members of the *Transcendental Club.* Club members met in the bookstore that Peabody owned for a period of time. She engaged in discussions with William Ellery Channing, a regular visitor in her bookstore, which influenced Peabody's philosophy.

Channing, a Unitarian minister, argued that intellectual freedom, moral freedom, freedom of inquiry, a belief in human virtue, and a respect for all persons were essential human values. These views were written around topics of women's rights and the abolition of slavery. Channing suggested that Peabody might want to publish these views in pamphlet format in conjunction with her bookstore. Peabody agreed but gave the pamphlets to an abolitionist group along with the rights and profits from sales (Snyder, 1972).

Peabody was impressed with Channing's views on the innocence and spontaneity of children. Central to his view was that each child was unique and should not be "molded" by adults (the idea that schools should "mold" children was common at that time). Adults, suggested Channing, were often too self-serving when considering children. In his view, the least desirable effects derived from schooling came when teachers dominated.

He argued that dominating children was not compatible with good education. Domination, according to Channing, ignored the child's consciousness and reduced the capacity for self-understanding and self direction. Discussions with Channing influenced Peabody's ideas about the value of early education.

Peabody, anxious to get started in teaching, accepted the job of assistant teacher to Bronson Alcott in an experimental schooling venture. As an assistant to Alcott in the *Temple School,* Peabody, in a role a she enjoyed, recorded descriptions of one method employed in Alcott's early experimental classroom.

> About twenty children came the first day. They were all under ten years of age, excepting two or three girls. I became his assistant to teach Latin to such as might desire to learn. Mr. Alcott sat behind his table, and the children were placed in chairs so far apart, that they could not easily touch each other. He then asked each one separately, what idea he or she had of the object of coming to school. To learn; was the first answer. To learn what? By pursuing this question, all the common exercises of school were brought up—successfully—even philosophy. Still Mr. Alcott intimated that this was not all; and at last someone said, "to behave well," and in pursuing this expression into its meaning, they at last decided that they had come to feel rightly, to think rightly, and to act rightly. A boy of seven years old suggested, and all agreed, that rightly actions were the must important of these three. (Cohen and Scheer, 1997, p. 73)

Alcott's Temple School, so named because it opened in a building previously used for religious meetings, gave attention to the ideas of children. This manner of teaching children was so radical for the times that newspapers printed stories of this experimental event.

By 1832, before hearing about kindergartens, Peabody was ready to start her own school. Elizabeth Peabody and her sister Mary founded a school for children in Boston. Horace Mann, a resident in the same boarding house as the Peabody sisters, was a Massachusetts state representative working on projects to improve the state's prison system. The Peabody sisters were naturally attracted to Mann because of shared interests in human rights. In the early 1820s, Catherine Beecher and Horace Mann joined to promote public education in the West before public schools existed there. This will be discussed more fully later in the text.

In 1835, Alcott published Peabody's written records from the Temple School, entitled *Record of a School.* In 1836 Alcott published a second record of Temple School, *Conversations with Children on the Gospels,* also written by Peabody.

Alcott's daughter, Louisa May Alcott, was home-schooled by her father, who brought in Ralph Waldo Emerson and Henry David Thoreau to share a role in his daughter's education. An intellectual in her own right, Louisa wrote an immensely popular novel, *Little Women* (1868), and a less popular novel, *Little Men* (1871); in 1868 she edited *Merry's Museum,* a magazine for young women.

In 1840, with financial assistance from William Ellery Channing, Peabody opened a bookstore in an old residence on West Street in Boston. This bookstore served as a gathering place for people who cherished books. This group included regulars like Margaret Fuller, George Ripley, James Freeman Clarke, Orestes Bronson, Jones Very, and Theodore Parker. For ten years, Peabody's bookstore was a home for Fuller's "conversations" and *The Dial,* a transcendental publication.

From shared interests and discussions concerning human rights, Horace Mann became romantically interested in Mary, Elizabeth's sister, and they subsequently married. Mann's marriage to Mary Peabody redirected his interest toward improving education. This was taking place about the same time that Peabody was losing interest in the bookstore and transcendental discussions, publications, and obligations of running a bookstore. It could be said that this period encompassed Peabody's "search for social clarity."

In 1859 Peabody met Margarethe Schurz, the founder of the first German-language kindergarten in the United States, at a social gathering in Boston. Attending with Mrs. Schurz were her husband and daughter Agathe. As Agathe socialized with other children, Peabody and other observers praised

Schurz for Agathe's mature and enchanting interaction with other children. Mrs. Schurz assured the group that kindergarten attendance should be credited with her daughter's maturity.

Kindergarten was a new word for Peabody, and Schurz gave such a vivid description of her kindergarten that it captured Peabody's interest. Peabody expressed this interest to Schurz, who later sent her a copy of Frederich Froebel's book, *The Education of Man.* Peabody was captivated by descriptions of Margarethe Schurz's kindergarten in Wisconsin, and Frederich Froebel's book (Snyder, 1972).

Motivated by the excitement of kindergarten ideas, in 1860, Elizabeth Peabody with her sister Mary Mann, opened the first English-speaking kindergarten in the United States at 15 Pinckney Street, Boston, Massachusetts. The following year, the Pinckney Street Kindergarten boasted Peabody and Mary as teachers, along with a French teacher and a teacher of gymnastics. There were thirty children in attendance. The room had plants and animals, and children learned to read, write, and draw; all in keeping with Froebel's kindergarten principles of *mother play, gifts,* and *occupations* (Liebschner, 2001).

By 1864, Elizabeth and Mary were writing and disseminating information about the kindergarten movement. "Kindergarten—What Is It?" appeared in the *Atlantic Monthly.* In 1864, Mary and Elizabeth published *Moral Culture in Infancy* and *A Kindergarten Guide.*

Peabody was starting to envision a larger role for the ultimate influence of kindergarten. Kindergarten as an early system of education and training designed to pass a young population into the hands of traditional education was too limiting for Peabody. Well-run kindergartens, thought Peabody, could revolutionize the current moribund system of graded education by infusing it with a concern for humanity.

The United States was experiencing a considerable measure of intellectual opposition to the Civil War, the extermination of Native Americans, and the enslavement of blacks (Bernal, 1987). What can our system of education contribute to discussions of these conditions? thought Peabody. Kindergarten should be more than a mere attachment to the front end of an already poor public educational system, she thought. Kindergarten provided an opportunity to refine the education of youth prior to an indoctrination of the rightness of economic disparity and racial and religious bigotry.

Peabody attempted to intervene when John Brown and his seventeen antislavery followers were captured at Harper's Ferry, Virginia, after their revolt. All participants in the uprising were sentenced to death. She requested an audience with the governor to plead for a reprieve for the last two men sentenced to death. The Governor of Virginia denied Peabody's request (Snyder, 1972).

Peabody also visited President Lincoln during the last days of the Civil War, and was impressed that Lincoln had given her time to express her concerns. The trip was less than pleasant when Peabody walked Washington streets. Here, she witnessed hundreds of black homeless families with children near starvation, cast out by plantation owners after the emancipation of families previously held in slavery.

Peabody was at a theoretical confluence between kindergarten providing a critical role in growing a humane national society or kindergarten as a lockstep appendage to a larger system of graded education. Two factors complicated Peabody's contemplation. The basic requirement for public school teachers was a modest completion of four years of grade school, but the public system of appointing teachers was so politically corrupt that at times even the modest fourth-grade completion requirement was set aside and replaced with one month of "professional" training.

Peabody, at a low point in her quest for a *real* kindergarten, thought that Friedrich Froebel, "The Master," could help her understand how to design a "true" kindergarten curriculum, one that enabled young learners to stand on their own when entering a public primary school. Peabody had been inspired from her reading of Froebel's philosophy of gentle guidance as explained in his *Education of Man.* With a deep desire to develop a *true* kindergarten, Peabody sought a deeper conceptualization of Froebel's *gifts, occupations,* and related kindergarten curricula. At her earliest opportunity, Peabody booked passage on a ship to Germany, and her first stop was Berlin (Snyder, 1972).

After arriving in Berlin, Peabody visited Baroness von Marenholz-Buelow, who had been a student of Froebel's and was selected by him as a liaison between kindergartners in Germany and his students in the United States. The Baroness maintained frequent communication with an ever-increasing number of kindergartens in the United States, especially those with German roots.

Here Elizabeth found just what she was looking for, a kindergarten run as Froebel would have had it. She was intrigued by the equipment, the soft, bright-colored, worsted-covered balls, the peg boards, the perforated cards for embroidery, the child appealing pictures. She loved the old folk songs the children sang and the singing games they played. Teachers trained at the source must be procured in order to have a successful kindergarten in America. Elizabeth invited Matilde Kriege, an outstanding student at the Seminary, and her daughter Alma, to go to Boston and become a part of the Pinckney Street Kindergarten staff. (Snyder, 1972, p. 46)

Peabody's trip to Germany was an educational exploration into the origins of the kindergarten movement. Her meager knowledge of the movement had come from reading Froebel's book, from Schurz's reports of her German language kindergarten in Wisconsin, and from her brief immersion in running a kindergarten for one year in Boston.

She was then ready to admit her mistakes and start anew. Her relatively short immersion in the kindergarten movement did not diminish her vision for young children with kindergarten experiences becoming a more compassionate adult population.

In 1907, a little more than fifty years after Peabody's pursuit of Froebel's vision for *real* kindergarten teachers and graduates, it survived as a continually maturing movement, securely embedded in public education systems. Nina C. Vandewalker, Director of the Kindergarten Training Department of the State Normal School of Milwaukee, Wisconsin, wrote in the *Sixth Yearbook of the National Society for the Scientific Study of Education:*

> Humanization of the child as a factor in the humanization of mankind cannot take place without increasing recognition of man's dependence upon the past with its achievements, which gives validity to faith; without the realization of a present replete with opportunities for loving service; without the allurement of a future that is radiant with hope. Such are the ideas and ideals of the third, and latest, conception of the kindergarten program. Those who are working consciously under its guidance believe it to be in accord with the best that modern philosophy and psychology have to offer to the teacher. They also believe that it is in accord with the principles of the Froebellian philosophy. (1907, p. 114)

Peabody traveled in Europe for over a year, making friends among kindergartners, observing in kindergarten centers, and encouraging the best trainers and teachers to come to the United States to teach and demonstrate Froebel's kindergarten methods. These invitations increased trips to the United States by European kindergartners, giving birth to Froebel training schools and professional organizations that resulted in a significant increase in kindergartens infused with Froebel curriculum.

By 1870, news of kindergartens had become widespread in major cites in the United States. Peabody gave lectures in Chicago, Cleveland, Detroit, and Milwaukee, attracting supporters, teachers, and organizers along the way. The quest for quality childcare created an almost instant success for kindergartens among the upper-income classes who wanted more than custodial daycare for their young.

Newspapers and periodicals were occasionally critical of kindergartens and published articles in an attempt to influence parents because they were willing to give up family influences on their child's Christian values to "strangers." Overwhelmingly, by 1890, the prevailing idea promoted in part by opposing newspaper articles, that kindergarten teachers were well trained in "scientific" methods originating in Germany negated some of the criticisms. By 1900, there were more that 100 cities in the United States with free public kindergartens.

MARGARETHE SCHURZ (1832–1876)

Margarethe Schurz was one of Froebel's first students to take his advice and immigrate to the United States. She founded a German-language kindergarten in Watertown, Wisconsin, in 1856. Also a first among Froebel's students to take his advice and start a kindergarten in the United States was Caroline L. Frankenberger, who opened a kindergarten in Columbus, Ohio, an adventure that was not successful (Snyder, 1972).

Schurz, as many German émigrés had done before her, settled in a predominately German community in Watertown. Here, she established the first German-language kindergarten in the United States. Starting with her own three children and gradually adding a few others, Schurz was true to the Froebel tradition by seeking to let it be known that she had been a student of Friedrich Froebel. From ideas acquired from her Froebel training, Schurz guided children in their artwork depicting home and village life. Art projects were coordinated with Froebel's songs and music in *Mother Play* and *Gifts and Occupations.*

Following Froebel's philosophical foundations, the kindergarten curriculum brought "mother" (the *teacher* in the symbolic role of mother) and child together in affection, trust, and cooperation. A major part of the daily curriculum were songs led by the teacher that identified classroom fixtures like the clock, plants, pets, the teacher's desk, etc. In kindergarten classrooms the teacher accompanied children's singing with piano playing or another musical instrument.

This musical experience integrated song with the child's physical self (for example, eyes, mouth, nose, ears). This part of Froebel's curriculum made the piano an essential musical fixture in kindergarten classrooms in major U.S. cities from the early 1900s through the 1960s.

Following the inclusion of the concept of the physical attributes of *self* in Froebellian curriculum, mother play would move to include in song, visible environmental objects like the classroom wall clock, table, chairs, and door, for example. These objects would be labeled in the classroom for children to highlight in their writing and storytelling.

The practice of labeling objects in the classroom environment is of Froebellian origin, and used later by others, like Montessori, for example, and is still practiced in some early-childhood classrooms today.

It is also true that, as late as the 1960s in the United States, influences of Froebellian curricula could be found in kindergartens throughout major cities like Chicago, Cleveland, Los Angeles, New York, Philadelphia, and San Francisco, just to name a few. As late as the 1970s, music as a major part of the kindergarten curricula required that university early-childhood majors gain proficiency on a musical instrument, preferably the piano, but often because of limited time and space, the recorder would be substituted. In the aforementioned cities, however, a piano was available in many kindergarten classrooms.

While Froebel educators brought their kindergarten philosophy methods, and materials to United States, it was inevitable that our ingenuity would orient the original kindergarten practices to make them more compatible to our way of life. Among the many variations made on the original Froebel model by kindergartners in the United States were large wood building blocks, the project method (discussed elsewhere in the text), and teacher after-school home visits to educate younger children remaining at home because of age or illness.

Thought to be one of the greatest developments in the toy world at that time, large building blocks became essential for all kindergartens and remain a staple in today's early-childhood classrooms. Building blocks create opportunities for girls and boys to exercise, defuse tension, enter group interactions to plan, build, and use blocks to expand their imagination and create a project.

Starting with the Schurz-Froebel initiative, early childhood teachers sought an understanding of *how children learn;* elementary school teachers concentrated on *what children should be taught,* such as math, science, etc. It is also true, in universities and colleges where there was a major field of study in early childhood, that the field often had the largest number of undergraduate majors when compared to other education departments. Following the combining of early childhood and elementary-education departments, the direct instruction of reading and mathematics (what children should be taught) eliminated music and many other essentials from early-childhood education.

In the 1990s, various state education agencies, whose policies must be followed by state universities, integrated early childhood education and elementary education. This move sequestered traditional early-childhood education to the education shadows. Today, early-childhood education and elementary education in many states are the same. A salvation for early-childhood education might rest in the current surge of interest in infant and toddler education.

The first kindergartens in the United States followed the Margarethe Schurz-Froebellian model. These kindergartens were independently separate from grade schools, and when they were located in public schools, kindergartners raised donations to pay rent to local school systems.

This "independence" was often uneasy for kindergartners in the presence of inquiring suspicions from their first-, second-, and third-grade colleagues. These tensions were felt in public schools and in universities where early childhood education and elementary education were taught as separate fields of study.

This problem has persisted whenever attempts have been made to merge elementary education with early-childhood education. In 1920, Alice Temple, a professor in the School of Education at the University of Chicago, defined the problem for her time and place like this:

> The problem of unifying the work of the kindergarten and primary grades is one that is engaging the serious attention of many teachers and supervisors. It was thought, therefore, that a description of the way in which one institution has attempted to solve the problem might have some practical value at this time.
>
> The following pages will give an account of what the School of Education has done, both in its college department and in its elementary school, to bring the work of the kindergarten into organic relationship with that of the rest of the school.
>
> During the first years of its existence the College of Education of the University of Chicago, like other teacher-training schools, offered in its undergraduate department one general curriculum for the training of elementary-school teachers and one special curriculum for the training of kindergartners.
>
> There are two chief reasons for the existence of this practice in normal schools. In the first place, the kindergarten was maintained in this country as a private and philanthropic institution for many years before it became a part of the public school system. . . .
>
> In the second place, the controlling principles, methods, and materials of the early kindergarten were so different from those of the early primary school that a special type of teacher-training seemed to be absolutely essential. (Temple, 1920, p. 498)

In a manner of speaking, the history of early-childhood education in the United States reveals kindergartens as a project more common to social activism. Through this notable activism, kindergartens were eventually accepted as a natural starting point for young children entering public education. Margarethe Schurz, founder of the German-language kindergarten, and Elizabeth Peabody, founder of the English-language kindergarten, framed a critical part of that history.

An essential aspect of kindergarten curriculum that has gradually disappeared from preschool and kindergarten curriculum is music. In this regard, the philosophy of Emile Jacque-Dalcroze became embedded in early kindergarten curriculum. Dalcroze demonstrated a philosophical approach to the teaching of music to young children as an experience for life (Andrews, 1954).

EMILE JACQUE-DALCROZE (1865–1950)

Born in Vienna of Swiss parents, Emile grew up in Geneva. His parents arranged exceptionally fine musical experiences during his early life. Geneva was the home of many world-renowned musicians and composers, and therefore, there was no lack of skilled teachers and performers to reinforce Emile's early musical development.

Later in life as an accomplished musician and conductor, he established relationships with well-known teachers, composers, conductors, and university professors. This created opportunities for Dalcroze to acquire knowledge and experiences in the philosophical and psychological foundations of drama, dance, theatrical production, and artistic performance, and to meet university faculty with specialties in teaching. During an assignment as conductor of an orchestra in Algiers, he became interested in the profound differences between basic rhythms in Arab music when they are compared to rhythms found in European music. While a music conductor in Algiers and a frequent visitor to indigenous performances, he gradually realized that the power of music could transcend the "irregular" rhythms of Arab music and the "regular" rhythms in the basic music concepts he was taught. This could be achieved, theorized Dalcroze, when individuals are in touch with their inner feelings and are able to achieve harmony between body and mind (Spectorm, 1990).

During his adult life, relationships with university professors and experts in various disciplines, along with his discoveries of indigenous rhythms, drew Dalcroze to an appreciation of the relationships between music, rhythms, body movement, and the human spirit. Later in life, as a teacher of harmony in the *Conservatoire of Geneva,* his observations of his students' performances encouraged him to infuse a stronger emphasis on emotion in their music (Findlay, 1971).

Because of this emotional awareness that he decided to instill in his students, he hoped that they would acquire a deeper sense of the relationship between time, tempo, rhythm, and themselves, rather than a mere mechanical reproduction of notes in striving for that "perfect" performance. Though their performances were done well mechanically, Dalcroze observed a lack of feeling and emotion in their musical renditions. If this lack of emotion in his students' performances came from an overtechnical music education (because teachers did not dwell upon the *feeling* of tempo and rhythms), thought

Dalcroze, it was an obligation of music pedagogy to expand music by making it an *education for life* (Andrews, 1954).

As suggested by Bachmann (1991), Dalcroze theorized music education as an education *through and into music*. Music in education, thought Dalcroze, could accommodate all students despite race, religion, class, or status in life. These concepts of an integrated music appreciation and performance might have occurred to Dalcroze during his stay in the African nation of Algeria. During Dalcroze's time there, Algeria had been under the colonial rule of France for almost a century (Naylor, 2000). Colonized Africans were viewed by the French and other Europeans as second-class citizens in their own country.

It was not uncommon that Europeans living in colonized countries (in this case Algeria) treated the native population as a servant class, and over time would discover "exotic" differences between their culture and the culture of the exploited countries. Differences in Arab rhythms would naturally attract the attention of Dalcroze because of his deep interest in music, not necessarily in Arabs.

Much to Dalcroze's credit, however, he positively valued his newly discovered Arab/African rhythms and defined them as important and necessary for European musicians to value rather than dismiss as "tribal" and of little value to the world community.

By 1920, practically all Froebel-oriented kindergartens in the United States included Dalcroze-style tempo, rhythm, and accompanied dance movements in their curriculum. They were introduced to the education community during the height of the progressive education movement (Dewey, 1902).

The 1920s appearance of young children dancing in bare feet on boxes, on the classroom floor, and on tables more than annoyed *traditional* educators, but "free" body movements in loose-fitting dresses, tunics, and skirts were attractive and energizing to *progressive* educators.

Such activities were teacher initiated and conducted to encourage free spirit movement and achieve individual harmony between mind and body. It was believed that collective harmony between individuals and groups could be achieved through individual consciousness (Findlay, 1971).

The inclusion of Dalcroze music experiences and accompanied interactive rhythms are completely absent from early childhood segments of K–12 programs in public schools today. *Eurhythmics*, however, still remain in various models of early childhood, but are seldom enacted (Hohmann and Weikart, 1995).

Dalcroze eurhythmic influences can still be found, however, in some curricula in a few privately sponsored preschool programs in the United States today, and are included in preschool programs on various levels in as many as 25 countries.

HORACE MANN (1796–1859)
AND CATHERINE BEECHER (1800–1870)

Horace Mann, a pioneer in public school education, joined a number of other outstanding educators from time to time to advance educational opportunities in the United States. It was not uncommon in the 1700s and early 1800s for men to be more healthy and robust than women. Many outlived several wives, each wife bearing four to eight children. And, it was not uncommon for the wives of farmers to have more than 10 children.

Catherine Beecher, a pioneer for improving family health and domesticity, worked to improve the education and well-being of mothers and their families. Her sister, Harriet Beecher Stowe, the author of *Uncle Tom's Cabin*, disagreed with her sister Catherine's opposition to voting rights for women and militant antislavery movements. Their youngest sister, Isabella Beecher Hooker, was a strong opponent of slavery.

Catherine Beecher had opened her first school for women in 1823, in Hartford, Connecticut. Here she promoted the idea that girls and boys should be taught the same subjects. With backgrounds in human rights, Beecher and Mann joined in a mission to establish common schools in the fast-developing western United States.

Beecher's primary goal was to improve the lives of White mothers and their daughters through good advice for changing their domestic circumstances. Mann was also concerned about domestic improvement, *but for all families.* He was a strong antislavery advocate, and this advocacy was combined with work toward the advancement of public education. At that time, public schools (public education) were referred to as "common schools" (common education).

Horace Mann's vision for public education in the West would start with the education of teachers. In the rough, male-dominated West, fewer women were attracted to teaching because women's salaries were one-half or less than men's. In Beecher's view, teaching was an ideal profession for young women because this profession could serve as a deterrent to early marriage. And, women as teachers would create a more nurturing classroom environment and elevate the idea of schooling in the public's view.

Beecher wrote several books on family domestic life aimed at informing women of ordinary matters concerning food, dress, and domesticity. She advised against layers of undergarments for young women, because such attire inhibited their opportunities to romp and run like boys.

Beecher was also an early supporter of offering both girls and boys studies in school related to home economics and mechanics (shop). These dual gender opportunities were not offered in public schools in the United States until the 1960s. She was such a domineering figure that projects started with her involvement or under her leadership were often continued by persons other than Beecher (Rugoff, 1981).

Among Catherine Beecher's published works are *The True Remedy for the Wrongs of Women* (1851), *Physiology and Calisthenics for School and Families* (1856), *Common Sense Applied to Religion, or the Bible and the People* (1856), *The American Woman's Home* (1869), *Woman Suffrage and Woman's Profession (1871), Miss Beecher's Housekeeper and Healthkeeper* (1873), and *Educational Reminiscences and Suggestions* (1874).

JOHN DEWEY (1859–1952)

Born in Burlington, Vermont, John Dewey is probably the most publicly known philosopher associated with fields of education. This is true for two important reasons. Dewey's writings on educational philosophy in the early 1900s sought to awaken educators and the general citizenry to the vast possibilities existing in systems that supported education. He thought that public and private schools should provide greater opportunities for pupils to participate in their own learning. Anyone who had spent time in a public school of that period could produce stories of stifling restrictions (Dewey, 1899).

Dewey's published works have undergone extensive reviews, interpretations, and learned discussions. Imagine the typical classroom teacher of the late 1800s, whose formal education seldom went beyond the fourth grade. Such a teacher would be unable to comprehend the writings of a philosopher like Dewey, whose works attracted scrutiny at the highest levels of academia.

Dewey's philosophy did not penetrate the educational establishment in a manner that could change public classrooms, and it was slow to create any significant improvement in public schooling. Despite this lethargy for change, Dewey's philosophy was gradually disseminated in a variety of other ways. Some schools were founded for the sole purpose of promoting an interactive learning environment between young children and their teacher through an interpretation of Dewey's writings. There were other schools that went beyond central ideas of Dewey, and they remain as monuments to the legacy of John Dewey. Many of those schools exist today. Outstanding examples are the Bank Street Children School in New York and The Peninsula School in California.

His ideas extended beyond education to a view of the world as a social system (Dewey, 1899). During a time when the United States was yet to achieve a democracy, Dewey joined W.E.B. Du Bois in 1905, along with Jane Addams, William Dean Howells, and Lincoln Steffens in northern New York to sign the original charter for the *National Association for the Advancement of Colored People* (NAACP). This movement was later joined by such notables as Albert Einstein, who frequented black communities in Princeton, New Jersey.

MARIA MONTESSORI (1870–1952)

Montessori's work with an impoverished group of children started near the turn of the century. It is generally accepted that she opened her first school, *Casa dei Bambini* (The Children's House), in 1907, in a slum district in Rome known as San Lorenzo. This was followed by additional school sites in Italy, and eventually in other parts of the world.

Montessori's stated objective for opening the first school in this location was similar to Oberlin's school, which had been established in a poor French mining community 140 years earlier. That was to offer free schooling for poor children whose parents could not, or would not, attend to the educational needs of their children.

A building in San Lorenzo was offered to Montessori to use for children by a San Lorenzo organization, the *Roman Association for Good Building*. The Lorenzo division of this organization owned an abandoned apartment building in San Lorenzo that they wanted to employ for a good cause while at the same time searching for an alternative use because it was often left unattended. The association surmised that Montessori could organize activities for a large number of children, who were, at the time, gradually destroying the empty apartments in their unsupervised play.

It was concluded that if children could be organized to gather in the otherwise empty rooms under the supervision of Montessori and her staff, the association would benefit from not having to restore the building as apartments for families, but continue it as a "school" to productively occupy the time of children who might otherwise be attracted to vandalism.

In the beginning of the 20th century in the United States, when the kindergarten movement was in its infancy, the works of Oberlin, Pestalozzi, Froebel, and Montessori were known to groups of activist women. These activists, many of whom had trained with Froebel or one of his students, were instrumental in the integration of kindergartens into grade schools, and their ideas shared a significant place in the kindergarten movement. Gradually, the works of Froebel and Montessori became most influential in early education curricula in the kindergarten movement in the United States.

By the time Montessori methods became well known, the work of Froebel was already deeply embedded in the kindergarten movement in many countries and had influenced thousands of teachers and children around the world.

In the United States, the name of Froebel was known by anyone associated with child development and learning.

Despite Froebel's early capture of the world's interest in kindergarten, it did not take very long for interest in Montessori to overtake Froebel's popularity. It was in 1907, through most media outlets of that time, when world news was broadcast about the Montessori "revolution."

Maria Montessori was an exciting personality who visited the United States in 1913 and charmed audiences with her grace and dignity. During that visit she directed her lectures to mothers, though her audiences included men. She did not speak English at that time but had an interpreter to explain her message to the audience following each six to eight minutes of lecture. The audience sensed that parts of her message were left out, because her interpreter took fewer than three minutes to interpret eight minutes of the Montessori presentation for the audience.

Despite this obvious omission, her audience of mothers and single women were impressed by what they were told. Montessori emphasized practical matters of knowledge. Her earlier experiences with teaching orphans gave her insight into what mothers should know to help them comfortably through motherhood. She described what all mothers needed to know to get them through their daily rituals. Procedures related to etiquette, standards of behavior, acts of kindness, common measures, and basic mathematics, such as shapes of objects and market packaging that came in shapes like squares, cylinders, etc., were presented. She explained to women that every home had simple objects that could demonstrate essential knowledge and concepts to a child.

For example, purchases from the market came in containers (squares, rectangles, etc.). And the shapes of common furniture pieces could be used as examples in teaching children things like comparisons and relationships. Her presentations were loudly applauded because persons who were not trained as educators could identify some important role for themselves in the lives of children.

After visits to various countries, Montessori trained teachers and enthusiasts who would start their own programs. By 1925, the state of Rhode Island had placed Montessori classrooms in all of its elementary schools, and Montessori training centers were introduced in various parts of the world.

Maria Montessori was the first woman to earn a medical degree in Italy. After qualifying as a physician, she was selected by her government to serve in several posts. Among her first assignment was assistant director of the Psychiatric Clinic at the University of Rome. In this position, one early assignment was to visit residential centers for the mentally challenged in Rome. During these visits she selected individuals most suitable for research to be conducted by Montessori with her colleagues in the university clinic.

Her visit to the institutions where orphans were housed changed her professional career. As was common in other countries, orphaned children were poorly clothed, inadequately fed, and often residing in squalid, overcrowded conditions. There were few health services and few attempts to educate orphaned children. Montessori's primary assignment was to provide mental health services, but she realized almost immediately that most of the children were also in need of individual attention and schooling.

Except for tabletops used for feeding, the environment of these centers for "insane" children was bare. The most common activity occurred after meals. Here, children scrambled over crumbs that occasionally fell on the floor. There were no materials designed for learning or objects of play to advance their knowledge. From her visits, Montessori concluded that the children's needs included mental health and a knowledge of the world around them. And their needs were more pedagogical than psychiatric.

From her contacts in the medical field, Montessori was made aware of the work of two French physicians, Edourad Seguin and Jean Itard. Their studies of children focused on those with special needs. Their reports informed the world about a group of learners who were otherwise ignored and often improperly treated. Montessori sought their knowledge to assist her with a clinical understanding of children who, at that time, were identified as mentally retarded.

From these early relationships with professionals in the field, Montessori was invited to present a paper at a pedagogical congress meeting in Turin, Italy, in 1899. This address was remembered for her main theme; children in Italy's mental institutions should not be viewed as outside of organized society, but children who should be educated in the same environments as "normal" children. By the 1970s, in the United States, this idea was brought to public schooling, and became known as *mainstreaming.*

Montessori's radical point of view led the Education Minister of Rome, Guido Bacelli, to invite Montessori to give lectures on the "feebleminded." These lectures were so well received that they ultimately led to the opening of a state Orthophrenic School in Rome. Children in the various day schools in Rome who demonstrated difficulty in learning with the standard curriculum were brought to this school. Children from the asylums, like those visited by Montessori, were also brought into the Orthophrenic School.

Montessori gradually organized and instructed the staff, and had meals prepared for the children (who were later taught to prepare their own), all the while observing the manner of work rendered by established rituals. During one of these observations, Montessori noticed one child sitting on top of a crate engrossed with an object that she was manipulating, pretending that it was a toy. The child's concentration on the manipulation of this make-believe play object was so intense that when the box on which she was sitting was moved, the child ignored the disturbance, and her concentration on the play object remained unbroken.

This was one of Montessori's early experiences with what she interpreted as the need for children in learning situations to have objects of interest to serve as manipulatives to support the learning process. After needs for attention to health and nutrition were satisfactorily met, Montessori set out to design materials that she thought would attract young minds to acquire skills in mathematics, reading, and language.

Another early act was to secure classroom furnishings like child-size chairs and shelving that was reachable for children. Each child was responsible for securing food on his or her plate, eating utensils, napkin, and locating a place at the table. After eating, each child washed his or her plate, utensils, and the area where he or she ate and placed the cleaned tableware on the shelf from which it could be retrieved for the next meal. In Montessori programs, rituals like mealtimes were used as teaching opportunities.

Over a period of time, Montessori taught the staff to understand methods and materials and how to introduce them to children and assign the next task. Because she viewed her objects of learning as needing *direction* from a teacher to a child, Montessori addressed each teacher as *directress.*

The directress was taught the purpose of the object, its age-related objective, how it was integrated into other activities, and what should follow it. In part, from her observation of the child engrossed in her singular attention to a play object, Montessori concluded that children as learners should work alone, not in groups. This idea was later to include small-group cooperative activities.

Montessori's methods are frequently taught in Montessori training centers in various parts of the world for the benefit of new teachers planning to work in Montessori programs, and those seeking a renewal.

Some results obtained in these centers were recognized as remarkable. Many children from Montessori schools in Italy demonstrated at public gatherings that they were able to read and write as well as average regular school children of their time.

Montessori returned to university studies specializing in philosophy and psychology. She was appointed the Chair of Hygiene, in Rome, at the women's college, and an examiner in the Department of Pedagogy. In 1904 she became head of the Anthropology Department at the University of Rome.

By 1910, Montessori's view that children thought of as slow learners should be integrated into the regular school classrooms became a topic of study by educators of special-needs children. Modern-day educators have accepted the idea that some Montessori methods and materials could be used with all children, and this has led to the presence of selected Montessori-type materials in many early-childhood and special-education classrooms.

The Lancaster System

In an effort to reduce costs associated with the daily education and supervision of large numbers of school children, a monitor-type system was employed. The most commonly used was called *The Lancaster System of Improvements in Education.* This system directed a teacher to assign more mature and sometimes higher-achieving students to supervise and sometimes teach groups of twelve to sixteen lower-performing students for the day, or tutor small numbers in a specific subject (Lancaster, 1821).

The framework for this economical approach to schooling was introduced by a London educator, Joseph Lancaster, and was quickly adopted by many school systems in the early 1800s. Lancaster drew his ideas for the monitor system from one used by the *Brothers of Common Light,* and other Jesuit study groups.

As schools for children in the United States adopted the Lancaster system, modifications were made to assign one adult teacher the ultimate responsibility for the first 200 students. These accommodations meant assigning student monitors to such tasks as recording pupil attendance, entering pupil grades in the school register, assigning new students to their classroom, and tracking and storing books and slates.

It was not unusual that 10 to 12 pupils selected as monitors could be observed "supervising" as many as 100 younger and/or lower-achieving pupils Except for the most rudimentary skills, schools failed to provide an environment that encouraged children to actively participate in their own learning.

The Lancaster system was employed in public schools for children in all grades. For various reasons, however, this system was most successful when monitoring pupils were over the age of fifteen. With the primary purpose being maintaining good order, young monitors were seldom successful with pupils their own age and older.

TRENDS IN THE EARLY CHILDHOOD FIELD OF STUDY

In 1924, Patty Smith Hill planned a major conference at Columbia University's Teachers College and invited professors, teachers, and practitioners from variously identified early-childhood programs to help resolve the confusing diversification in the field. From terms like daycare, nursery school, preschool, and kindergarten, this conference identified early-childhood education as the study of growth and development of children from birth to age eight. And, the variety of differently labeled practitioners were invited to identify early-child education (Zeitz, 1969).

In 1931, the *International Kindergarten Union* (IKU) and the National Council of Primary Education joined to form a learned society, the Association for Childhood Education (ACE). This association included nursery school, kindergarten, and primary education then located in K–12 schools. The IKU had embraced John Dewey's *progressive education* and directed its service area as children from two to eight years old.

Over time, the parent group, the ACE, accepted the scope of the International Kindergarten Union and changed its name to what it is today, the *Association for Childhood Education International*.

As interest in early-childhood education in the general population expanded, kindergarten classrooms have gradually appeared in all public schools in the United States. This has meant an expansion of programs for university colleges and schools of education.

The state of Georgia, for example, did not require its public schools to have kindergartens until 1985. Gradually, this expansion has meant the suppression of early-childhood education under a broadened umbrella of elementary education, creating an education model with a range from kindergarten through grade six. In some state systems, teacher training in the early childhood grades are ignored, while grades four, five, and six are emphasized. This often results in early-childhood curriculum becoming very similar to curriculum in grades four through six.

In 2006, universities are attempting to resolve this conundrum by ignoring the fundamental differences between early-childhood education and elementary education. At the university teacher-training level, students who elect major study in early-childhood education are often taught by professors with elementary-education training, hired to teach early-childhood courses and supervise the early-childhood practicum. Such money-saving strategies add to confusion in the field and jeopardize the credibility of universities where these lines are blurred.

Planners and practitioners in the field of early childhood entered the field in part because of an attraction to the age group, others because of an interest in theories of developmental psychologists, like Sigmund Freud (1856–1939), Jean Piaget (1896–1980), Erik Erikson (1902–1987), and Lev Vygotsky (1896–1934). In this group, Dewey is the only philosopher/teacher and social activist; the others were psychologists. Originally denied a presence in public schools, infant schools and kindergartens were promoted by social workers and social reformers.

The Settlement House Kindergartens

The settlement house movement, led by Jane Addams, Jacob Riis, and Lillian Wald, was designed to provide a variety of social services in early 1900s tenement neighborhoods that became home for European immigrants and southern migrants. How to apply for employment, how to participate in local and national elections, and studies for citizenship, dance, and music were offered. Services for kindergarten-age children, usually conducted by well-trained social workers, were included in these community-based activities. Abigail A. Eliot, the first woman to receive a doctorate from the Harvard School of Education and Director of the Ruggles Street Nursery School in Boston, opened that nursery school in 1922. She remarked later that:

> Each of us in the early nursery schools came out of a different background. I was a social worker. After I graduated from Radcliffe I worked as a social worker in Boston. But I did have the unusual opportunity of studying and working in England for six months with a woman I would call the founder of the nursery school movement: Margaret McMillan. So I really do have some training as a nursery school teacher. (Hymes, 1978–1979, p. 8)

The name *nursery school* was originated by Margaret McMillan in England, where she opened an infant school for orphans and children of the street. Here she established a large open-air nursery school in a low-income section of London, providing daily health inspections, food, clothing, and outdoor activities. McMillan's work was started in 1911 in the Deptford section after England's health studies of 1908, 1909, and 1910 reported that 80 percent of children were healthy at birth. At school entry, however, only 20 percent were in good health.

McMillan's work was recognized as an important contribution toward the health and development of London's poor children. In many ways McMillan's popularity stimulated a public demand for nursery schools. For example, *The Fisher Act* was passed by the British Parliament in 1919 providing grants to public-initiated nursery schools that cared for children two to five years of age.

Such services were federally supported in the United States during World Wars I and II. There were, however, several nursery school teachers in the United States who took the opportunity to study at the McMillan Nursery School and Training Center in London. This was an attractive opportunity for kindergartners and nursery school teachers in the United States to study and improve their craft.

In this regard, *The Women's Educational Association,* while operating a Montessori School in Boston, was asked to take over the Ruggles Street Nursery

School in the Roxbury Section of Boston. Not having much specific experience in running nursery schools, the Woman's Education Association, after learning about McMillan's training center in London, sent Abigail Elliot to McMillan's Center in London for training.

In 1922, after her training in London, Abigail Eliot returned to the Roxbury section of Boston to run a school at 147 Ruggles Street. On her first day, she was greeted by 30 children ranging in age from a few weeks to 14 years. She was surprised to find a well-cleaned facility with a few Froebel and Montessori educational and play materials, unused and tucked away in a closet. Several other nursery schools were starting up in other areas of the country about the same time.

During the same month, Edna Noble White, another nursery school pioneer in the United States who had studied at Margaret McMillan's Center in Deptford, opened the Merrill-Palmer Nursery School in Detroit, Michigan. Edna Noble White's academic credentials were in the field of home economics; this was a common background for nursery school professionals.

The most prominent neighborhood houses were the Henry Street Settlement in New York City, founded in 1893 by Lillian Wald; Hull-House, which opened in 1889 in Chicago; and the Williamsburg Settlement House, opened in the 1960s in the Williamsburg section of Brooklyn, New York.

Four years after its opening, Hull-House, under the leadership of its founders, Jane Addams and Gates Starr, opened the first community-based kindergarten in Chicago. The settlement house movement was pliable enough to respond to community crises as they arose. For example, thousands of immigrants and southern migrant families arrived in the northern cities between 1890 and 1920, usually with two to seven children. Ten years after their arrival, the children of immigrant and migrant families were having children. This led to the need for a great number of settlement house services to satisfy the needs of poor children.

There were pressing issues in neighborhoods, cities, and statewide in the nation. For example, settlement houses provided kindergartens, recreational, and music programs for children in neighborhoods. Child labor conditions were exposed to state legislatures and at the national level to the Children's Bureau, a federal agency that investigated and reported on the exploitation of children under pressure.

It became commonplace that activists in the kindergarten movement were often supporters of other social causes and actively participated in the forming of such activist groups as the NAACP, the American Civil Liberties Union, voter education, child labor reform, and workers rights.

The leadership and the workers in settlement houses were mostly educated in fields of social service and social work, not education. The first kindergarteners in settlement houses were supervised by social workers. This gave community-based settlement house kindergartens a greater emphasis on neighborhoods and families than one would commonly find in public schools of that time.

Public schools viewed the newly arrived kindergarteners as an add-on to their already planned primary grades. The newly educated kindergarten teachers brought with them a new curriculum somewhat unlike that in current use by teachers in public school primary grades. Families with school-age children were accustomed to grade-focused student needs, and this model did not encourage parent involvement.

Public Kindergarten

Susan Blow (1843–1916), almost fifty years younger than Peabody, grew up in a wealthy St. Louis family. Though well respected and a member of the upper class in Boston, Peabody could not match the wealth of Blow, but respect for Peabody's decisive approach to work was high among kindergartners. They were both supporters of the Froebellian kindergarten movement and invested their energies to expand its influence. While Blow, before launching a project, would take time to evaluate how its plan should be carried out, Peabody could be impressed with an idea, start work on the project immediately, and work out the details along the way.

Starting in the early 1900s, several schools for educating kindergarten teachers were opened in various parts of the United States. Some were formed as an extension of the curriculum for the emerging "Normal School" systems (Harper, 1970). Others were integrated into university teacher-training departments like home economics. Yet others were started as separate programs in teacher colleges, as was the case at the University of Chicago and Columbia University Teachers College in New York.

Independent centers for the education of kindergartners were founded by successful students of Friedrich Froebel and others who were merely adherents to his curriculum. Maria Kraus-Boelte, a graduate from Froebel's kindergarten school in Germany, opened a kindergartner-education center in New York City. During Elizabeth Peabody's visit to Germany, she was successful in recruiting Froebel-educated Baroness von Marenholtz-Bulow, and her daughter Matilde Kriege, to relocate in the United States to teach Froebel-inspired kindergarteners. Susan Blow had been encouraged by Elizabeth Peabody and William Torry Harris, St. Louis School Superintendent, to study kindergartener education in New York City, the center of Froebel education in the United States at that time.

After completing work at the New York Institute for Kindergartners under the tutelage of Maria Krouse-Boelte, Susan Blow returned to St. Louis, where she had previously requested permission from Harris to work in one of the newly planned public kindergartens in that city.

Peabody, seeking every opportunity to promote the kindergarten movement, visited cities to give talks to book clubs, education groups, and learned societies, and wrote letters to influential persons in public education. William T. Harris was one of the notables to whom she wrote. Aware of the national prestige of the St. Louis school system, Peabody's letters encouraged Harris to add kindergartens to his already well-known educational system.

Peabody had been corresponding with Harris for some time, describing the merits of kindergartens and how they would benefit the St. Louis public school system. At that time there were no public kindergartens in the United States.

It was Harris, after hearing about Susan Blow's completion of Froebellian kindergarten training in New York, who encouraged her to return to St. Louis and teach in his proposed kindergarten program. The insistence by Peabody in her letters to Harris that he should introduce kindergartens in St. Louis was an additional encouragement.

> Superintendent Harris' concern was with the sad fact that most St. Louis children attended school between the ages of seven and ten. He saw in the kindergarten not only its intrinsic value for the early years but a practical means for the children of St. Louis, since there was little hope of holding many in school for a few more years of education beyond the age of ten. Accordingly, he recommended to the Boards of Education that some kind of classes be established for children below seven. The board responded by appointing a committee to study the advisability of adding "play schools" to the public school system. The success of the "play schools" established by Dr. Adolph Douai, the respected German educator in Newark, New Jersey, was a contributing factor to the decision of the Board. (Snyder, 1972, p. 61)

It is also true that, during the mid- to late 1800s, the St. Louis School System, under the leadership of Harris, was changing its curriculum to satisfy a reshaped philosophy. These changes, and the academic future unfolding for St. Louis, were being carefully observed by school districts throughout the United States. This high interest was due in part to the reputation of William Harris. Harris was a conspicuous leader, serving in highly respected posts in well-respected educational and learned societies, and was one of the most influential leaders in the field of education at that time.

> During this period, school officials reshaped their philosophy of education; schooling designed to nurture intellectual and moral development was pushed aside in order to maintain an agenda favoring work and citizenship training. The

traditional academic curriculum could not advance the new program, many believed, as a massive curriculum restructuring followed. Significant changes in the student population paralleled the revisions of philosophy and curriculum .(Graves, 1998, p. 182)

The kindergarten curriculum of Susan Blow adhered strictly to her own Froebel German education. Among other things, it included music, "gifts and occupations," mother play, storytelling, and discussions of Greek myths, Shakespeare, Dante, and Faust. Blow was the first to establish meetings with mothers and group trips to cultural sites. Gradually, teachers in the elementary grades were adapting kindergarten activities to enhance their classroom activities.

After gaining a place in public schools, kindergarten educators perceived that the integrity of their curriculum was under threat from teachers and administrators who were trained in elementary education (grades 1–6). Kindergartners took the unique philosophical stance that emphasis should be placed upon the child's *transition* from home life with mother to schooling with a teacher. Further, the kindergarten curriculum should include play, music, and songs, caring for plants and pets, and literature from Greek tragedies, the *Odyssey*, and Shakespeare's works.

The schools in St. Louis, observed Blow, were no exception to a gradually emerging threat from elementary educators who were intent upon replacing the Froebel philosophy with a curriculum of direct instruction and rote memorizations of the times table, word lists, and related paper-and-pencil seat work.

Blow supervised kindergarten teachers in the St. Louis public school system and helped to plan their approach to work. She carried out these duties without pay during the period that William T. Harris was superintendent. She left this post when the St. Louis School Board of education relieved her of the supervision of kindergartners and placed it under elementary education. Kindergarten teachers who were employed with Blow resigned to protest the transfer of kindergarten supervision to an elementary education–trained supervisor.

Being among the most respected Froebellian-trained kindergartners in the field, the resigning St. Louis kindergartners were recruited for prestigious positions in the northeast. Cynthia Dozier became Supervisor of the New York Kindergarten Association; Laura Fisher became Director of Boston Public; Caroline Hart became head of The Training School of the Kindergarten Association of Baltimore; Harriet Niel became Head of The Training School Kindergarten in Washington, D.C.; and Mary D. Runyan became head of the Kindergarten Department at Teachers College, Columbia University (Snyder, 1972).

This exodus created a major event in the kindergarten movement. It represented a dissemination of public school kindergarten ideas from Missouri to wider parts of the United States. This transition also expanded the influence of Froebel's ideas for early education and provided greater protection for early-education curriculum when faced with elementary-education forces.

These events also influenced other cities to experiment with kindergarten programs in a variety of ways. Between 1880 and 1885, John Swett, Superintendent of Schools in San Francisco, established two "experimental" kindergartens. By 1886, Swett opened more kindergarten classes and established kindergartens as a permanent addition to the San Francisco School System.

In 1874, Susan Blow moved to Boston and joined a kindergarten movement first started by Elizabeth Peabody. At that time Boston was a thriving community for kindergarten activists with interests in transcendentalism, women's suffrage, anti-lynching, and Native American rights. In 1884, William N. Hailmann, as school superintendent in LaPorte, Indiana, established kindergartens in 1888.

By 1875, a group of Froebel-educated kindergartners had become active on the West Coast. In 1878 the San Francisco Public Kindergarten Society was founded, along with the opening of the first free kindergarten in California, the Silver Street School. Its first students came from an impoverished community known as Tar Flat. By 1890, in the city where kindergartens were inaugurated in its public schools, kindergartens had grown to approximately 90.

Early in the 1900s, a surprising number of regular teachers in small communities had less than six years of formal schooling. Inevitably, the widespread interest in early-childhood education and development continued to increase on university campuses around the country, and academic requirements and certification were continually enhanced.

Montessori and Dewey Meet

In 1913 Maria Montessori, who by that year had been written about extensively in newspapers worldwide, arrived in the United States with her Italian interpreter because she understood little spoken English. Dewey attempted to integrate his active-learning philosophy with what he knew about the more broadly envisioned Montessori perspective.

Promoted as a method that encouraged children to actively participate in their own learning, Montessori suggested that her method was designed precisely to free children to enact their own potential for *self-development.* The Montessori system provided the external means necessary for natural growth. This "natural growth," according to Montessori's literature, takes place in three parts: *sensory, intellectual,* and *motor.*

Jean Piaget's philosophy of best practices in enabling the knowledge acquisition of young learners shared some of the fundamental ideas about the role of educators in this process with Maria Montessori. Both Montessori and Piaget focused on the *role of the teacher* in describing their visions for promoting learning and development. Their writings also focused on learning objectives that should occur when their teacher/child practices are followed.

Piaget and Montessori differed as to how the relationship between teacher and learner should be constructed. In Montessori's theory, the *directress* (teacher) is trained while attending a Montessori Training Center. It is this training that informs preteachers and directresses who return for renewal on the nature and needs of children. The graduates, after returning to their classrooms, would enact their competence in the role of a directress. The directress would use Montessori-designed materials for promoting child development and learning and make incremental assignments. Assignments that followed were designed to build upon what had been previously learned.

According to Montessori, this process starts with the child following instructions provided by the directress, who at the same time introduces the child to activities and their related devices. These are the means by which children *participate* in their own learning, according to Montessori, who also explained that under the directresses' observations, learners were enabled to *teach themselves* in a prepared environment (Orem, 1974).

Piaget, on the other hand, theorized that in the teacher/child relationship, the teacher should prepare an environment appropriate for the child's needs and interests (Dewey, 1916). However, children should be free to select the subjects and objects to be studied in promoting knowledge acquisition. Dewey insisted on learning objectives and outcomes. The learner should be encouraged to select, search, investigate, and interpret, with informed guidance from the teacher. The teacher, in turn, has clearly defined objectives and expectations for learning, and guides the learning toward the prescribed objectives and expectations (Dewey, 1938).

We now know that all learning starts with a learner's sensory system (vision, auditory, taste, smell, and touch). Impulses received in a sensory system are passed on to our central nervous system (CNS). The CNS comprises the spinal chord and the brain. *Attention* is a central factor in learning in that, in the absence of attention, an experience would not likely penetrate the sensory system, and that is the first stage (Morgan, 1997, p. 43).

When Maria Montessori and John Dewey met, Dewey wanted to establish a cooperative relationship with Montessori programs to integrate his ideas with the Montessori model. Dewey made what he thought was a single request for a simple change in the Montessori classroom design that would allow the child more freedom of choice, with fewer powers invested in the Montessori-designated directress.

On this point, Dewey never reached an agreement with Montessori. From her point of view, the power of the directress was essential. In Dewey's view, the history of education in the United States demonstrated that total power and control in the hands of classroom teachers (in this case, the Montessori's directress), demonstrated too few opportunities for children to make real choices and participate in their own learning.

Dewey was on a crusade to change the fundamental nature of restricted classrooms in the United States and envisioned a place for the Montessori Model in that crusade. Montessori's motivation for developing a model in the first place had been driven by her experiences with developmentally challenged youth, among them children who were raised in impoverished, delinquent-prone environments.

Through her interpreter, Montessori emphasized in her response to Dewey that there were important reasons for seeking directresses and not traditionally trained teachers for her classrooms. Montessori and Dewey failed to reach an agreement, and the academic world at large experienced this loss.

Despite this failure of Montessori or Dewey to compromise, as of this writing there exist hundreds of Montessori organizations, facilities, associations, societies, teacher-training courses, institutes, parent groups, and clubs, as well as international, national, state, and regional study groups, along with numerous Montessori classrooms around the world.

It is also true that Dewey is celebrated as an advocate for progressive education where children participate in organizing and acquiring their own knowledge (1916). There are hundreds of university-based John Dewey Societies and public- and private-school teachers who openly identify with Dewey's philosophy. There are philosophical societies and other learned groups affiliated with existentialism and phenomenology who study writings related to works of Dewey. There is also a John Dewey special-interest group in the *American Educational Research Association.*

Dewey's sense of personal social and moral obligations was integrated with his quiet social activism for human causes. In this regard, he participated in the founding of several institutions and learned societies promoting equal opportunity and betterment for all humankind. During his work toward social change, Dewey was among the original founders of the *New School for Social Research,* the *American Civil Liberties Union,* and the *American Association of University Professors,* and he was a charter member of the first teachers' union in New York City.

Today, many contemporary learned institutions like *Bank Street College,* along with hundreds of teachers in public school classrooms, and numerous private grade schools like the *Peninsula School* in California, the *Walden School,* and *Bank Street Children's School,* in New York, and *Summerhill School,* in Saxmundham, England, were inspired by the philosophy of John Dewey.

2

Theoretical Perspectives

Our task is not to suppress the specialization of knowledge but to achieve harmony and truth over the whole range of knowledge. This is where I see the trouble, where a deep-seated disturbance between science and all other cultures appears to lie. I believe that this disturbance was inherent originally in the liberating impact of modern science on medieval thought and has only later turned pathological.

—Michael Polanyi

For this writing, a theory is a systematic principle(s) that explains human behavior and can be verified by empirical investigations. For example, Freud describes childhood behavior in steps and stages. Freud's first stage of early development is the *oral* stage. There is *empirical* evidence that supports this aspect of Freud's theory. Infants demonstrate an oral response to objects that touch on their mouth or in the general area of their mouth. This behavior can be *observed* and *recorded* by anyone investigating the behavior of infants. This observation, therefore, can demonstrate *empirical* evidence that supports Freud's *developmental theory* as it pertains to infants as being sound.

Theorists who have influenced studies of early-childhood education and child development include Ivan Pavlov, Sigmund Freud, Lev Vygotsky, James Watson, Jean Piaget, Erik Erikson, and B. F. Skinner.

IVAN PETROVICH PAVLOV (1849–1936)

Born in Ryazan, a small town about 100 miles from Moscow, Ivan Pavlov was expected to follow tradition and become a priest like his father. For a while Ivan did study at the Ryazan Ecclesiastical Seminary. During his seminary studies in the 1860s books on Western theory and philosophy written in the Russian language were starting to appear. It was during this time that Pavlov discovered the writings of Charles Darwin, including Darwin's theory of evolution. This discovery of Western thought was a life-changing experience for Ivan Pavlov in that he decided not to follow a career in the priesthood, but rather enter the University of Saint Petersburg to study mathematics and science (Windholtz, 1991).

Ivan Pavlov is credited with discoveries associated with *classical conditioning*. In the 1890s, while still interested in Darwin's theory of the individual pursuit for existence, Pavlov attempted to integrate Darwin's theory with his studies of animal reflexes associated with their digestive systems. Conducting these experiments with graduate students and sometimes with Pavlovian adherents, who by that time numbered in the hundreds, discoveries were made that confirmed connections between animal neural systems and their cerebral cortex during their salivary response (Pavlov, 1927). Confirmation of these behavioral influences encouraged Skinner and Watson to experiment on applications for human learning (Watson, 1928).

Pavlov's proposition was confirmed during his laboratory work in the 1890s while exploring animal digestive tracts. He theorized that the upper and lower digestive tracts had a different response to foods of different texture. Here, salivary tracts differed in secretion when foods were moist as opposed to foods that were dry. With animals to study, and foods like meats and breads involved in the studies, a bell rang to note specific animal feeding time, a task that was performed by lab assistants.

By now, most university students in their first year of psychology study the work of Pavlov that led him to discoveries of *behavior modification*. It is the story of the behavior of dogs being fed at the same time that they heard the sound of the bell. When the bell sounded without their being given food, the dogs also salivated because they associated the sound of the bell with receiving food. In the original ringing of the bell without the serving of food, the dogs rendered a neutral response and did not salivate. It was only after the coordination of bell ringing and feeding occurring several times, that this discovery was made.

In the early 1900s, S. G. Vul'fson, while a graduate student, was assigned to Pavlov's experimental labs at the *Institute of Experimental Medicine in Saint Petersburg*. He confirmed Pavlov's theory of neural animal responses to activity in their digestive tracts. This gave rise to a theory of connections between thought and behavior. Since that time, theorists have defined learning as *a change in behavior.* Behavior modification and operant conditioning, though developed by others like B. F. Skinner, E. R. Guthrie, and James

Watson, were drawn largely from ideas associated with Pavlov's *classical conditioning.*

Studies have also been conducted to determine the extent to which certain infant behaviors are more related to behavioral conditioning than to stages of development. Stage theorists (Freud, Piaget, and Erikson, for example) suggest that acts of behavior are developmentally influenced in part by one's environment. This has been an area of interest for investigators. For example, one study substituted a tone for the contact of a feeding nipple on the lips, to usher in an infant's expectation for feeding. Here, instead of following the assumption that an infant's oral response was a natural developmental reaction, the experimenter attempted to demonstrate that the infant's food searching behavior could be triggered by the presence of external objects, like the sight of a bottle or the mother's smile to stimulate the sucking response (Sameroff and Cavanaugh, 1979; Lipsitt and Kaye, 1964). Such studies have reported results that are important for an understanding of infant behavior, but they are less convincing as a challenge to the stage theorist's identification of the innate oral reflexes as infant development.

Theories of Watson, Guthrie, and Skinner are referred to as *behaviorism.* To proponents of behaviorism, theories of development are less relevant to knowledge acquisition, because in their view, the major human forces associated with learning can be encouraged by human responses to actual behaviors. In this regard, responses can be encouraged or extinguished. It is the pairing of a desired behavior with a positive stimulus that creates retention or rejection.

It is important to note that the work of behaviorists is based largely on observations of animals like dogs, rats, and sometimes birds, as in the case of Skinner. One human experiment of James Watson's involving a young boy brought strong negative criticism from his audience. On the other had, the work of stage theorists and developmentalists came from observations of human behavior. In the case of Piaget, his early works were descriptions of interactions with his own children during early stages of development (Table 2.1).

Behaviorists suggest that when young learners display a behavior, adults can respond *approvingly* or *disapprovingly.* When learners receive approvals, they are more likely to repeat those approved behaviors. Theories of behaviorism raised doubts about the significance of stage theories. Freud, Erikson, and Piaget theorized that child development emerged from a gradually unfolding process under the influence of the environment (Baillargeon and DeVos, 1991). Behaviorists theorized that actions identified as developmental could be called forth with appropriately selected stimuli (Watson, 1928; Skinner, 1953)

Table 2.1.   Stage Theorists

Age	Object Relationships	Caregiver-Child Issues	Psychosexual Stages	Psychosexual Stages	
			Freud	Erickson	Piaget
0–3 mo.	none to reflex; 3 mo. smile	initial adaptation			
3–6 mo.	mother preferred	reciprocal interaction	oral stage	basic trust vs. mistrust	
6–9 mo.	stranger anxiety	early directed activity			sensori-motor stage
9–15 mo.	exploration and differentiation	vocalization	anal stage	autonomy vs. shame and doubt	
12–18 mo.	beginnings of self-awareness	self-awareness			
1–2 yr.	exploration and differentiation of relationships between self and others	initial testing of destructive aggression	phallic stage	initiative vs. guilt	preoperational stage
2–3 yr.		modification of aggression			
1–3 yr.	consolidation of body image and beginnings of sex identity	extension of secondary process functions in interaction			
3–6 yr.	consolidation of sex identity; genuine concern for others; self-control	development of concern for parents first as extension of self, then as separate people; differs as to sex	oedipal stage		
6–9 yr.	competition and achievement; differentiated manner according to sex and age of object	concern turns outward, to school, community, peers	latency	industry vs. inferiority	concrete opera-tions

Skinner did not think that one should wait for behaviors to unfold but that desired behaviors could be elicited. Some aspects of behaviorism can be recognized in many of today's classrooms. Behaviorism is at work when teachers apply incentives like gold stars, high grades, words of praise, positive comments on student's commendable work, etc.

Skinner theorized that learning could be achieved through the method of pairing behaviors with selected stimuli (Skinner, 1953). He described negative and positive reinforcement. Here, the nature of the reinforcement would determine the extent to which it would be perceived as negative or positive. This interpretation by the learner would determine the extent to which an act by the teacher could reinforce or extinguish a particular child behavior. Skinner theorized that negative reinforcement or punishment could extinguish undesirable behaviors, when positive responses to selected behaviors could encourage positive behaviors and extinguish negative ones (Skinner, 1938, 1957).

The suppression of certain behaviors could be interpreted as punishment by some observers, and not by others. It is this aspect of behavior modification that brought criticism from stage theorists and developmentalists (Table 2.1).

By the 1920s, following the work of M. K. Perova, one of Pavlov's more promising students, Pavlov blended his own work into psychiatric studies of neurosis. Others in the field, like Freud in Germany, were moving along the same experimental path. This appeared in Freud's earlier search for *a scientific psychology*. Freud abandoned this "search" when his close colleague, Wilhelm Fliess, discouraged Freud's work in this direction because he thought that it was a wasteful pursuit (Masson, 1985).

By the 1930s, Pavlov was observing patient behaviors in the neurotic and psychiatric clinics in Leningrad to determine the extent to which psychosis and neurosis could be understood through theories of neuronal activity. The clinical approach to treatment for chronic symptoms of neurosis assumed that patients were "weak" and therefore likely to acquire neurotic symptoms after they perceived a series of experiences they defined as social assaults.

Pavlov's approach to studying these conditions theorized that environmental stress could overwhelm the patient's inhibitory process. According to Pavlov, two possibilities existed for chronic symptoms to occur, and a "weak" temperament existed for either to emerge: one, symptoms of "weak" individuals of the *thoughtful* type, labeled *psychasthenic neurosis,* and a different set of symptoms for "weak" individuals of the of the *artistic* type, labeled *hysterical neurosis* (Pavlov, 1927).

Freud, in his search for a *scientific psychology,* centered his interests on the function of the neuron. Pavlov, shortly thereafter in his study of neurosis, followed the same pathway of study. Freud's mission, however, focused on a larger view of creating a scientific image for psychology. Pavlov, on the other hand, studied the function of neurotic behavior while accepting the nature of psychological studies as empirical pursuits. Pavlov rejected the idea of psychology as a science (Morgan, 1997).

During the late 1800s, philosophers in England and Germany were looking to psychology as the area of discourse from which a coherent theory of knowledge and logic could emerge. It was a period when philosophers, psychologists, and scholars of scientific thought were attempting to apply the rigors of scientific methods to complex problems of logic. This period of advanced thought in philosophy and psychology has been identified by various scholars as the emergence of a new psychology for that time called *psychologism.* (Morgan, 1997, p. 12)

SIGMUND FREUD (1856–1939)

Freud's theories were employed by psychotherapists in Europe and the United States. Categorized as *psychosexual,* Freud's theories of child growth and development framed the foundation of the work of psychotherapists and child psychologists from the late 1880s to the 1950s. During this later period, child psychotherapy practiced in Europe and the United States was Freudian influenced.

At the same time, the work of Jean Piaget, a psychologist, was receiving attention on an educational/child developmental track, from interests expressed by those in early-childhood education. Piaget's work is classified as *psychosocial.* Piaget started with observations of childhood intellectual responses to questions on the nature of matter and how things worked. As with Freud, Piaget's work began to attract educators and psychotherapists (Table 2.1).

Erik Erikson, who had been a student of Freud's daughter, Anna Freud, is important to any discussion of Sigmund Freud and Jean Piaget because works by these three psychologists were reported as dynamic steps and stages in child development. Erikson, however, described his stages, as did Piaget, in *psychosocial* terms. The patterns of development described by each theorist have become over time a basis for a considerable number of empirical studies (Erikson, 1950; Ginsburg and Opper, 1969; Strachey, 1961; Uzgiris and Hunt, 1973).

Maria Montessori, a contemporary of Piaget and Erikson, also reported a theory that described steps and stages of growth and development. This theory survived in the background of Montessori's teaching, in that it appeared only when necessary to reinforce an understanding of her practice. Montessori focused on age from a perspective of physical competence and social awareness of the child. Activities designed for teaching and learning in Montessori classrooms took into account capacities of children that were generally expected based on age and maturation. This perspective served as a theoretical framework for Montessori's age related performance expectations for students (Cole, 1950; Edelson and Orem, 1970).

Early-childhood classroom teachers who were educated in colleges and universities prior to the 1970s have been taught an academic content that includes a historical early-childhood framework, sociological and psychological foundations of early childhood, and a practice derived from a 100-year-old tradition. This traditional training prior to the 1970s focused on *how children learn.*

Elementary-education classroom teachers who were educated in colleges and universities post-1980s, and students currently in those programs, are educated along the same lines as elementary, middle grade, and high school teachers. This group of teachers, sometimes erroneously called early-childhood teachers, performs well, but their focus is primarily *what children should be taught* (Morgan, 1999).

Today, in too many university-based early-childhood teacher education programs, planners have been blending the title "early childhood" with "elementary-education" approaches. Such blended programs have ignored significant traditions of early-childhood education, its rich theory, history, and sound philosophy, while concentrating primarily on *what children should be taught.* This approach provides too little attention to the foundations of child development found in the theories of Erikson, Freud, Montessori, Piaget, and Skinner.

Freud's theoretical framework explained that all life passes through prescribed stages of growth and development. This development is directly influenced by individual relationships between the child and significant others. Here, Vygotsky's theory of a *zone of proximal development,* though not psychosexual, is compatible with Piaget and Erikson's psychosocial perspectives. Freud's psychosexual theories are guided by sexuality and gender and are developmentally based.

Because the word *sexual* had taboo connotations in public discourse in the late 1800s, negative criticism came from the general public. The idea that Freud maintained too great a concentration on sexual issues was also the view of others, like Carl Jung and Erik Erikson, for example. Critics expressed the view that Freud concentrated too heavily on sexual aspects of growth and development, when in reality Freud ocassionally implied *gender* when addressing issues related to sexuality.

Several aspects of Freud's writings were misinterpreted by Freudian adherents. Among them his use of the term *unconscious.* It is my interpretation that it is likely that Freud meant *subconscious.* I offer this suggestion because for one to be *unconscious,* one would have to be in a deep sleep. Surely, Freud intended to mean that the *conscious level* was not in play here as the primary source of one's communication. But the level of consciousness that came forth in the voice was resting elsewhere in the individual's memory. And issues denied expression were nonetheless stored in memory. Epistemology of that time probably left too few word choices for Freud to provide clarity for his emerging ideas, some of which were laced with social taboos.

The unconscious was Freud's way of explaining how two strongly opposing personality traits could exist in the individual's personality at the same time. Only one would have a *voice.* The stronger trait would gain expression by repressing the opposing trait. The opposing trait would rest in the unconscious and not achieve expression. In the late 1800s, the idea of a subconscious was one of Freud's contributions to psychology (Gay, 1988). Borrowing ideas from early African (Aesop), and Greek (Plato, Socrates) philosophers, Freud theorized an *unconscious* (subconscious) existence of ideas available in the human memory system that represented conflicting views; here, *one view* achieved representation in the expressive personality by repressing its *opposing view.*

Early poets and philosophers proposed this "conflict of mind" in the context of several parables, the most common among them being the Biblical tale of Adam and Eve. Here, because of the chosen acts of Adam and Eve in the Garden of Eden (original sin), all future humanity inherited a basic choice between *divine commitment* and *carnal pleasure.* And, once a choice is made, the remaining choice was assumed to rest beyond human consciousness—in the *unconscious.*

This concept receives attention in many undergraduate psychology texts when discussing Gestalt psychology. A graphic representation of two faces is presented in a manner that makes them also appear to be a vase. An observer can attend to the *two faces* in the picture or an image of a *vase,* but the observer cannot attend to both the *faces* and the *vase* at the same time (Morgan, 2003).

It is also true the word choice in describing his work was a concern of Freud, especially in conversations with patients whose behavior he was encouraging them to modify. In his frequent face-to-face encounters with colleagues, patients, public media, and various audiences who were ready to act upon his spoken and written word, the wrong word could betray his intended meaning.

It was not until the late 1950s that sexual differences could be discussed or written about openly in professional education literature. As late as the 1970s, print media outlets maintained a list of words that were taboo, not to be spoken or printed in public media. One example of a public media taboo is the word *lousy.* Though not opposed in print today, the idea that there existed somewhere a list of taboo words had a chilling effect on public media to the extent that publishers shied away from words that they *suspected* were taboo. This often meant that professional discourse and print media shied away from mentioning important biological differences between girls and boys.

It was common knowledge within various professional groups and to a lesser degree in the general public that sexual differences between boys and girls existed in chromosomes, internal organs, external sex organs and genitals, as well as various secondary sexual characteristics.

We can now freely discuss that boys are stronger than girls when strength is viewed in the physical sense. However, more often than not in emotional matters, males can appear weaker. Boys tend to display more psychological symptoms when parents divorce. It is also true that at birth and throughout life, males have more developmental problems and are more vulnerable to injury and disease (Freud, 1961; Baumrind, 1986).

According to Freud and Piaget, developmentally, children do not fully understand sexual differences until after the age of four or five. For Piaget, it is a stage of the awareness of concrete matters (Piaget, 1954). For Freud, it is the end of the oedipal stage and the beginning of sexual latency. Freud describes the sexual awareness of children openly, while Piaget's references to this period focus on the child's understanding of asexual environmental matters. In this regard, while Piaget focused on the child's emerging awareness of animal classification, such as the fact that a dog is different from a horse, Freud explained a developing sexual attraction toward their mothers by young boys (Piaget, 1954; Freud, 1961).

While some professionals view Piaget's reports as more helpful in practices associated with schooling and classroom practices, there are others, like school psychologists and social workers, for example, who consider an understanding of a young boy's longing for his mother (that cannot be fulfilled because her time is captured by his father) helpful in resolving some deep-seated behavioral problems (Freud, 1954).

Family members are often interacting in close proximity to one another and share many encounters like mealtimes, lounging around the TV, and related activities, and this makes it reasonable that attractions occur. As a society we maintain an emotional rejection of the idea that a mother, father, sister, brother, uncle, grandmother, or grandfather can be sexually attracted to one another. Freud suggested that such attractions were normal, and he made the concept a part of his seduction theory. This concept is related to and can be observed as an extension of Freud's theory of *internalization* (Masson, 1985).

To guard against outward manifestations of sexual encounters between children and adult members of their family, society has established in law and taboo against such practices. Harm can also occur when the taboo has the effect of producing adult denial and whispers, rather than open discussions among parents, teachers, and other professionals prior to the incident(s). There also exists a variety of sexual encounters within families; though identified as incest by professional therapists, they are not illegal according to statute (Forward and Buck, 1979).

Freud theorized child development from life experiences described by his adult patients. By now, even the general public is aware of Freud's "couch" in a therapeutic setting where he encouraged his patients, from a relaxed supine position, to discuss matters that came to mind. From time to time, these matters included experiences from their childhood. It was during these sessions that Freud was able to pair childhood descriptions from his patients with memories of his own childhood and observation of children in his environment. Weber provides an insightful description of Freud's dynamic concept of sexuality in child development.

> The stages were not perceived as completely distinct and ages of transition varied, but the dynamics grew out of Freud's position on infantile sexuality. Responses to the child's behavior in these stages were alleged to be decisive in the development of personality; this was considered particularly true during the first three stages, which covered the first four or five years of life. The oral stage, with the libido localized in the mouth and oral regions, dominated the first months when the infant was dependent upon the mother. Proper oral gratification became linked to the manner of feeding and weaning. Around the age of two the second stage began with libidinal pressures moved to the anal region, thus making the process of toilet training significant to personality development. A repressive regimen produced far reaching effects, according to Freud, as responses gained at this time were generalized in later behavior. The important aspect of the phallic stage (3–6 years) was the resolution of the Oedipus complex. The strength of the super-ego came into play to form the bulwark against incest. These three significant stages of early childhood were to be further resolved in the subsequent latency and genital periods in which socialization grew and interest became focused on others. (Weber, 1984, pp. 110–111)

Differentiated responses to babies by others usually start with the label *boy* or *girl*. Everyone from parents and siblings to strangers will treat infants differently according to their sex label (Matlin, 1993). Boy babies are often dressed in blue and girl babies in pink, and this sets the stage for different treatment by significant others. In one study, an infant girl was dressed in neutral clothing, and responses to the infant differed as to the sex that the observer attributed to the child (Brooks-Gunn and Matthews, 1979). *Gender* refers to the *social* implications of being male or female. *Sex* refers to the *biological* implications of being male or female.

Confrontations with colleagues because of sexually oriented theories occasionally brought Freud's work under a bright light of public attention. Early in his career from observations in the children's ward in hospitals it was apparent that some children under the age of seven had been sexually abused by male family members. Freud, from an assessment these observations, prepared a paper theorizing observations resulting from these disturbing discoveries (Gay, 1988).

Within the context of child growth and development, Freud integrated his observations of what was apparently incest with his existing theories of seduction. He viewed this new paper integrating his observations with his theory of seduction as a major breakthrough. If presented well to the right audience, Freud surmised, it might serve to convince skeptics of his psychosexual theory related to childhood developmental age-related stages (Freud, 1961; Masson, 1985; Gay, 1988).

The response from the audience drawn from a society of psychotherapists, of which Freud was a member, was rejecting and completely unexpected by Freud. The audience rejected Freud's hypothesis as well as his report of adult male sexual assaults on children. Freud reported later that "my colleagues have abandoned me." This experience had such a profound effect on Freud that he changed his previously published *seduction theory*. This new explanation identified the child as the subconscious perpetrator (Masson, 1985; Gay, 1988).

After he received a stunning rebuke from his colleagues, Freud changed his seduction theory from his earlier analyses to a theory that sexual abuse described by his adult patients was either imagined or actually desired by them, especially when they were children. When this sexual desire was not fulfilled, according to Freud's revision, the child as an adult recalled an imaginary event.

We can recast Freud's *seduction theory* here. Freud's earliest working model proclaimed that some male family members sexually abused female children. Later in life, when conflicts arose for women who had not resolved memories of such experiences, they would likely seek therapy from Freud or his professional colleagues. Freud's paper, in part, was a signal to his colleagues concerning the predicament created for such women when therapists rejected their accurate remembrances (Masson, 1985).

From Freud's perspective, sexuality involves drives of reproduction and human mating, and this calls for socially approved courtship, mating, and human reproduction. It is commonly agreed in the field of psychology that reproducing one's self is a basic drive, and this is one dimension through which the psychological structure of life is framed (Bailey and Pillard, 1991). Freud theorized that human interactions were resolved by our mental capacity to understand and accept the process of human reproduction. In his view, we are prepared for this process through experiences with significant adults, starting at birth and gradually developing through our childhood.

Stages left unresolved remain in the unconscious (read *subconscious*) of individuals until they are resolved (during therapy) or ignored. Occasionally, a minor unresolved issue might "break through" during an encounter, and we might remark, "Oh, that was a Freudian slip" (Freud, 1965). Dissimilarities between a child and a single parent would render different developmental conflicts than if that single parent and child were of the same sex (Freud, 1965; Bell, Weinberg, and Hammersmith, 1981).

Freud described the stages of individual characteristics from birth that are followed by a sexually inspired pathway of an *oral stage, anal stage, phallic stage, oedipal stage,* and *latency*. Freud's psychosexual stage theory is theorized in chronological age ranges with designated accompanying behaviors. Freud's descriptors can be matched with the *psychosocial* stages described by Piaget and Erikson. In Freud's *Psychosexual Theory*, the *oral stage* can be recognized through observations of the infant's behaviors.

The foundation of Freud's theory is based on three sub-sections of personality, the *id, ego,* and *superego*. According to Freud's theory, the *id* is that part of our personality that contains basic human sexual energy that strives for satisfaction. There is an unresolved subconscious tension that builds around an individual's emotional and physical needs (Freud, 1954, 1965).

For educators, these three aspects of personality can be explained best through examples of *mental processes* that can occupy a period of time almost too short to measure:

Examples

Let us imagine that at the start of a school day, a child enters her assigned classroom and finds that she is the only person in the room. After selecting a seat and putting her personal belongings aside, she recognizes a neatly wrapped sandwich on the desk next to her. Her first inclination is to take the sandwich and put it in a place where she can retrieve it later to satisfy her hunger. The ownership of this food will satisfy a basic need for *security* and *possibly survival* (hunger drive). This is an example of the *id* in action (concern for self).

In the next stage, a few minutes later, the same student, *through her sense of self*, will conclude that if she takes ownership of something of value that does not belong to her she will be identified as *dishonest*. The ego has a desire to self identify as an honest person and therefore, should not deprive the owner of the property (sandwich). Being deprived, the actual owner would not be able to satisfy her/his needs if their property were not returned (concern for others). According to Freud, the ego is the *rational, realistic* part of the personality.

In the final stage, it would occur to her that someone could let it be known that a sandwich was taken. This awareness could be followed by her fear that others in the class would suspect that she was the first to arrive, and likely the guilty person. This knowledge would point suspicion in her direction, and this episode might end with the class identifying her as a dishonest person. *The superego is preoccupied with how others value us.* The drive for a positive evaluation by others might win the day if the *superego* is strong enough to *protect the ego by overcoming the id.* Here, the *superego* aspect of the personality acts as a "wise parent" enforcing conscience, social norms, and a sense of morality.

Here the *superego* is of particular significance for students of early childhood development because Freud theorized that the superego, in a variety of ways, provides a protective barrier for children shielding them from *incest* (Weber, 1984).

Incest is often viewed by the general public as an abhorrent (or aberrant) behavior that is common to bizarre people with distorted personalities. In reality, incest has been found in all racial and socioeconomic groups. It is also true that both women and men impose a variety of sexually abusive experiences on their sons, daughters, and other close relatives.

Researchers have identified two basic types of incest. The most well-known act of incest is illegal; this type involves sexual intercourse between relatives within a family. There are a great variety of other types of incest that Freud found among his patients; some were not illegal. A great variety of sexually abusive acts between close relatives exists today and many remain legal (Forward and Buck, 1979).

Studies suggest that girls more than boys are seduced into sexually abusive experiences, and when incest does not involve sexual intercourse, children are sometimes not aware during the time of the act of incest in which they are engaging that it is psychologically destructive. The most common acts of incest involve fathers and daughters, mothers and sons, grandfathers and granddaughters, mothers and daughters, fathers and sons, and siblings (Forward and Buck, 1979).

Sigmund Freud, Jean Piaget, and Erik Erikson are considered *stage theorists* because their ideas about growth and development are articulated in a chronological, age-sensitive, progressive manner of steps and stages. In several instances, the age markers of these three theorists are similar, but the developmental descriptors differ. The descriptors are designed to match each theorist's overall theory.

For example, Freud identified the *oral stage* as starting at birth and extending through 12 months. And Freud's oral stage is parallel with Erikson's stage of *basic trust vs. mistrust*, starting at birth and extending through 12 months. In Freud's view, the helplessness of newborns places their survival in the hands of caregivers who perform various acts of child care that contribute to their survival. Feeding is among the first acts performed by an adult for an infant. This establishes the point of our food intake system (mouth) as that aspect of the body that is the most sensitive until during future stages the human system develops basic motor skills and knowledge that enable us to participate in our own food procurement.

If during this period of basic trust/mistrust the infant's food needs are severely interrupted, the developing infant will carry these unresolved features to the next stage, continually seeking a resolution. If the trust/mistrust stage is resolved in *mistrust*, the individual could be left with a *basic mistrust* of others into adulthood, where in the more extreme cases, it might be difficult for this adult to sustain a relationship (Erikson, 1950).

In Erikson's theory, there is an expansion of the child's *oral-sensory mechanism*. In his broader view, feeding contributes to the infant's development of a trusting relationship, and the caregiver is identified with that trust (Erikson, 1950).

Starting with the neonatal period (0–12 month stage), smiles are prevalent during the first three months, and because of the organism's anticipation for feeding, facial areas around the mouth are super sensitive. Within the next three to six months, the infant's relationship with objects and other persons shows initial development, with a preference demonstrated for mother. And within the remainder six to nine months, anxiety around strangers is demonstrated. Strangers are persons who through their physical appearance or odor are not recognized by the child as a provider.

As previously mentioned, from birth to 12 months of age, in Erikson's *Psychosocial Theory,* infants develop *basic trust vs. mistrust,* depending upon the extent to which the environment satisfies essential needs to instill in the developing child a trust that essential needs will be satisfied. This same age range is described in Piaget's *Psychosocial Theory* as the *sensorimotor* stage (Piaget, 1964).

Erikson's theory identifies the ages of 9 to 15 months as the stage of *autonomy vs. shame and doubt.* During this period, children explore differences in objects in their environment, develop vocabularies, and become aware of a self that is different from others. Freud's *phallic stage* spans ages 12 to 36 months. It is a period of exploration with efforts to differentiate relationships between self and others. This is a consolidation of body image and the start of sexual identity. Children of this age will likely experience some modification and testing of developmentally emerging aggressive behaviors.

The period of 12 months to 36 months in Erikson's *psychosocial stage* calls forth childhood behaviors associated with *initiative vs. guilt,* suggested by Piaget as the *preoperational stage*. It includes a consolidation of sexual identity, self-control, and a concern for parents first, followed by a concern for others.

Freud, Piaget, and Erikson all agree that the age range of six to nine years can be set apart from all others. This period represents Freud's *latency stage,*

Erikson's stage of *industry vs. inferiority,* and Piaget's stage of *concrete operations.* In this stage there is a drive for competition and achievement that can be observed in different modes according to sex. Each of the three theorists indicates that during this age span, the concerns of the developing child turn outward from the family toward others, such as the neighborhood environment, school, community, and peers.

These interactions, according to Freud, are often influenced sexually by society's expectations (and requirements) for individually assigned roles and the individual's capacity to enact these roles in their social system.

Sex-role expectations for men and women in the 1800s were significantly different from the same set of permissions and expectations in the 1900s. For example, it was not until the 1900s that most men and women thought that women had the knowledge of or interest in the right to vote in national elections.

According to Freudian theory, ideas of rights and privileges are sanctioned by sex-based arguments. Imagine a female child's sense of self that might emerge from the realization that she will *never* be as knowledgeable or competent as her male counterpart.

According to Freud, realizations by children start to occur very early in life. In an age-related, developmental progression, growing children must negotiate their relationship with the parent of their own sex as well as their relationship with the parent of the opposite sex (Freud, 1961).

Freud implies an analogy here by describing the sexually influenced relationships between parents and their children. Freud names the age period of three to six years of age the *oedipal stage.* This name is derived from ancient Greek mythology. In this mythical tale, Oedipus unknowingly killed his father and married his mother. Freud suggests that during the phallic stage, the male child will get revenge by symbolically cutting off his penis. In healthy family environments, the male child resolves this conflict by identifying with the father's values, morals, and self-control.

> A little boy will exhibit a special interest in his father; he would like to grow like him and be like him, and take his place everywhere. We may say simply that he takes his father as his ideal. This behavior has nothing to do with a passive or feminine attitude toward his father (and toward males in general); it is on the contrary typically masculine. It fits in very well with the Oedipus complex, for which it helps to prepare the way. (Freud, 1965, p. 46)

Problems can emerge, according to Freud, when the male parent is absent and male children are denied the opportunity of a father figure in whom to exhibit a special interest. For girls, Freud suggests that they can be jealous of their mother because they want to possess their father. These feelings can rise to an anxiety level because of an emerging fear that she (the child) will lose the love from both parents (Masson, 1985; Bach, 1946).

Male and female children repress their sexual desires and resolve conflicts associated with the oedipal stage. During the latency period, six to nine years of age, there is a natural repression of sexual impulses until the onset of the genital stage. During this period, mature relationships are formed after the onset of puberty (Freud, 1961).

A childhood spent with a single parent could create a set of challenges and expectations that would differ from two-parent arrangements. In this experience, the sex of the absent parent or adult mate would significantly influence the child's experiences (Bach, 1946). Relationships are also expanded when the child's interests turn outward from the family, like being enrolled in pre-school. Here, childhood experiences are expanded beyond the family. More often than not, conversations with peers, experiences in viewing media programs, and friendships demonstrate and display a model of *two parents* in the homes of most children (Bach, 1946; Bailey and Pillard, 1991).

Today children have many opportunities for healthy growth beyond such experiences. During Freud's time, however, many children faced negative reactions when they socialized outside of family in neighborhood, school, and related encounters. Urie Bronfenbrenner described these social forces in his theory of human ecology, which is framed in a psychosocial pattern (1986).

Prior to the 1960s, psychologists tended to dismiss the work of Piaget because it was drawn primarily along qualitative lines from observations of children, some of which were his own. After careful examinations of his work and empirical comparisons of his conclusions with those of others, today Piaget's work has been accepted, respected, and even praised among early-childhood professionals (Beilin, 1992).

Though educated as a biologist, today Piaget is often identified as a child psychologist because his theories inform the practice of many teachers and psychologists. Like Friedrich Froebel, Piaget identified the child's own initiated *action* rather than the child's *thought* as the primary force in the child's intellectual development. Piaget sought to identify developmental structures that were present in child growth and development that were also true for the species. From that perspective, his work was not that of a psychologist but a genetic epistemologist, concerned primarily with human patterns of development that extend over long expansions of time (Ginsburg and Opper, 1969).

Born in Neufchatel, Switzerland, Piaget published his first scientific paper at the age of ten. It was a one-page description of an albino sparrow. He received a PhD in biology at the age of twenty-two. Within the next ten years, Piaget published more than twenty papers on various subjects in biology. He was also employed in several psychoanalytic clinics and laboratories in Europe with Eugen Bleuler, Theodore Simon, and Cyrl Burt.

This period is thought to mark Piaget's interest in early-childhood development, because his wife gave birth to their first son. In the early 1920s, Piaget was hired to work in the laboratory of Theodore Simon to scale a test that had been developed by Cyril Burt, on the reasoning of young children. It was the work of Piaget that was done for Simon and Alfred Binet that led to the construction of the first intelligence test (Ginsburg and Opper, 1969).

While working in Binet's Paris laboratory, one of Piaget's assignments was to develop a French version of several English tests of reasoning. Piaget had studied the works of Freud and Jung. Influences from this exploratory work led to Piaget's stronger fascination for a test taker's *reasons* for wrong answers, rather than the test taker's *correct* answers per se. This perceptive thoughtfulness found its way into Piaget's later observations of *how* learners think, rather that *what* learners think (Piaget, 1954). This conflict is at the foundation of today's disagreements between education planners of early-childhood education and their counterparts in elementary education.

As made explicit by Jerome Kagan, Piaget's perspective is derived from his self-identity as a genetic epistemologist. Epistemology, a branch of psychology, is a discipline that examines the origins of knowledge. Piaget's concentration on genetic theory is derived from his university studies in biology with a concentration on *human development*. Like Freud's and Erikson's, Piaget's theory is described in age-related chronological stages.

> Piaget's conception of infancy, like Freud's was influenced by debates on the mechanisms of evolutionary change. Piaget sided with those who wanted to award most of the power for change to the organism's commerce with the environment rather than genetic mutations. Piaget likened the development of cognitive function to the evolution of organs and bodily processes because, in his conception, the infant's cognitive abilities derive from active interactions with objectives in the world and from successive combinations to new challenges. When Piaget looked at the infant, he saw a baby playing with the mother's face and fingers. Nursing, being nurtured, and exploring the caregiver's fingers are all characteristics of infancy. It is not obvious that one of these functions is more central; theory awards one of them more status than others. (Kagan, 1984, p. 29)

Piaget posits that *thinking about knowledge* occurs at all stages. The acquisition of new knowledge at all stages, however, requires a framework that is acquired as knowledge during on-going experiences. *Organization,* according to Piaget, is required for *logic* and *reasoning.*

Let us say, for example, that a 36-month-old white child discovers an African American family in the market and wonders why there is a difference in their skin color when compared to the skin color of his family and many family friends. From this early discovery of color differences, the white child might assume a superior status for the color brown (because of his favorite crayon color and his preference for chocolate ice cream). He could wonder why his family is not a crayon or ice cream color. At this stage of development his *logic* is derived from his knowledge of color and how he *thinks* about the concept of color through experiences common to that age group (Anisfield, 1984).

When learners have attained Piaget's stage of *concrete operations* (approximately six years of age), their logical thinking is more advanced, and this would enable the child in our previous example to think about the nuances of skin color in common with greater maturity. The complex public meanings of race and color will become integrated with objects like crayon, ice cream, and people. True concepts of objectivity and logic will occur as the child makes meaning from experiences in family, with peers, and in child care, for example. As children make meaning, personal environments help shape maturity. It is sometimes true that developmental differences are reported when European children are compared to children in the United States, for example. Piaget's theories have been studied by others, and some have reported variations (Piaget, 1964; Baillargeon and DeVos, 1991).

Thinking, according to Piaget, is more organized in adulthood than in childhood. He identified *assimilation* and *accommodation* as the stages during which young learners achieve the ability to first accommodate new information, then assimilate that information into their previously achieved knowledge.

When accommodation and assimilation of new information cannot be integrated into the learner's cognitive system, *disequilibrium* will occur and require additional external cognitive experiences that enable the learner to accommodate the necessary information. According to Piaget, when the learner is capable of accommodating and assimilating, the disequilibrium will be relieved. Lev Vygotsky (1896–1934) described a similar occurrence in the absence of the terms like *accommodating* and *assimilation* (Piaget, 1954; Vygotsky, 1979).

LEV VYGOTSKY (1896–1934)

A Russian-born psychologist, Vygotsky is recognized for his *sociocultural theory* of child growth and development. His theory emphasizes a transfer of values, skills, and culture through social interactions between young children and their more knowledgeable associates.

Vygotsky suggested that learners make their meaning while being exposed to natural social interactions that evolve from child-child and adult-child experiences in family and community. As the current population matures into adulthood, this developmental process prepares the continually emerging population to perpetuate common values. This marks the essence of Vygotsky's theory of child development (1979).

He identified play as creating significant interactions that provide opportunities for the transfer of knowledge, along with personal and community values. We also note that play was an essential part of the curriculum in schools for young children established by Pestalozzi and Froebel. While Froebel, Pestalozzi, and many other kindergartners integrated play into the regular academic day and in a manner idealized this activity, Vygotsky theorized that play provides opportunities for the learners' self-selection, enabling expanded opportunities for learners to practice what they know and acquire new knowledge in the process.

Through a focus on play as enjoyment or a source of developmental aggravation, Vygotsky defined a role for play that was in general a rather trivial contributor to knowledge acquisition, compared to Froebel or Pestalozzi. For example, Vygotsky suggested that the view of *play* described by some theorists as a self-choice enjoyment did not become a joy for Western children if they happened to lose a game that they were *playing,* for example:

> To define play as an activity that gives pleasure to the child is inaccurate for two reasons. First, many activities give the child much keener experiences of pleasure than play, for example, sucking on a pacifier, even though the child is not being satiated. And second, there are games in which the activity itself is not pleasurable, for example, games predominantly at the end of preschool and the beginning of school age that give pleasure only if the child finds the results interesting. Sporting games (not only athletic sports but other games that can be won or lost) are often accompanied by displeasure when the outcome is unfavorable to the child. But while pleasure cannot be regarded as the defining characteristic of play, it seems to me that theories which ignore the fact that play which fulfills the children's needs result in the pedantic intellectualization of play. (Vygotsky, 1978, p. 92)

In early childhood, play can be discussed from perspectives that take into account its physical features. Such features can contribute to physical development because of the child's self-selected activities like climbing, skipping, hopping, running, and marching, for example. Other aspects of play can contribute to the inner emotional world of a child's contemplation and self-acquired meaning, as theorized by Froebel (1900).

To Vygotsky, it was trivial and unnecessary to separate play from the great variety of experiences during childhood (1978).

The most well-known concept of learning and development attributed to Vygotsky is his *zone of proximal development* (1978). This can best be described as the *learner's environment* when occupied by objects, events, peers, and more mature individuals. He theorized that an essential *zone* within which learning takes place can occur smoothly and spontaneously as the learner shares experiences with peers and superiors who are likely more mature. The learner follows this shared experience with his or her own attempts to participate in daily rituals.

On the first try, tasks like creating a bow after tying one's shoes or writing one's name will not be models of perfection, but over time if interest (or need) is maintained, and if getting along in society demands it, the skills will be accomplished. Experiences will occur for the learner that will involve verbal explanations by peers, along with a demonstration of how such skills are acquired, sometimes after clumsy attempts, failures, and retrying.

These are simple examples, but this concept of development following performance and the acquisition of knowledge involving Vygotsky's *zone of proximal development* can be understood when observing a child advance from family-only interactions to the stage of being capable of managing the complex nature of outside-the-family peer relationships. In Vygotsky's words, "Instruction marches ahead of development." Individuals can create their own zone of proximity and learn from sociocultural experiences.

Vygotsky integrated *development* and *learning*. His work defines these concepts in various domains. Some of Vygotsky's most significant learning and development theories have implications for language acquisition and thinking. Vygotsky theorized development from a *sociocultural* perspective (Vygotsky, 1979).

Lev Vygotsky was not alone in linking social experiences with learning and development. Albert Bandura (1991) and Urie Bronfenbrenner (1979), among others, associated developmental learning with social and cultural influences, and this is also true of John Mark Baldwin (1897), to a lesser degree.

Bandura's *social learning theory* (1977) suggested that the acquisition of knowledge and associated development can be acquired efficiently through the observations of others performing tasks. He termed the process of building one's knowledge through observations of others *observational learning*. One can hear the resonance of Vygotsky's *zone* in Bandura's *social learning*.

Bandura suggested that observers particularize what they select from their environment. He also suggested that observers select those behaviors that will produce rewards if repeated, and those behaviors that do not elicit negative consequences if reproduced (Bandura, 1977). Thinking along this track shares some features with the works of Ivan Pavlov, B. F. Skinner, and J. B. Watson that are discussed elsewhere in this text.

Social learning theories also frame the foundations for adult learning designed to encourage changes in their behavior. For example, young soldiers who enter the military services are often reluctant to kill the enemy. They are trained through a variety of approaches to overcome this reluctance. These teaching/learning sessions are designed by practitioners skilled in *social learning principles.*

In the movies of the 1920s and 1930s men were shown wearing hats indoors and out of doors to "teach" male viewers that wearing a hat when dressed was the "sophisticated" thing to do. This filmed visual also encouraged women to accept, and hopefully support, this male act, and was paid for by the apparel industry. Currently, we have witnessed an increased number of cigarette smokers in films. This is done to "teach" a new population that smoking is desirably sophisticated despite restrictive bans on this unhealthy, habit-forming act. These are expanded examples of why there exists belief in *social learning theory* by those who shape public opinion. An expanded view can be found in Bronfenbrenner's human ecology because his ideas imply our *environment at large* and are not limited to child-parent home and the immediate neighborhood as suggested by Bandura and Vygotsky.

SOCIAL LEARNING THEORY AND CHILD DEVELOPMENT

Verbal skills are enhanced through thinking and reasoning, and such skills are defined as elements of the *cognitive process.* As Bandura continued to refine his social learning theory as to how children acquire and develop knowledge, he explained that through attention to a "model" (significant others like parents and older siblings, for example), children remember their observation through recalling a model's behavior. This is followed by contemplation by the learner of the benefits and burdens of repeating the observed behaviors. Verbal skills progress through experiences developed along the lines of social learning. Some have called it *imitation* and/or *habituation.* When the Bandura model was fully developed it was called the *cognitive social learning theory* (Bandura, 1986).

Urie Bronfenbrenner (1979) proposed a social learning model he identified as the *Ecology of Human Development,* and this was explained on four interactive levels. Each level included a description of age-related access to institutions like child-care centers, schools, religious institutions, and similar socially visible and accessible entities. Each institution as a possible object in a person's life, along with the social experiences that occur within it, enacts its own particularized impact on the child's learning and development.

An ecological study of child development is an approach that observes the relationship between the child and society and identifies significant encounters with which all children in our society must interact.

These interactions are framed by the requirements of our social systems. For example, some families might seek to enroll their four-year-old child in a Head Start program. Other parents, sometimes going through a divorce, might send their four-year-old to live with a grandparent, while another four-year-old might remain home until required school attendance at the age of six, in the first grade.

Experiences for four-year-olds can be predicted with moderate accuracy, because of child laws, regulations of society through social policy, the accessibility of community institutions like churches and preschools, and realities of blended and regular families. These options are available for all four-year-olds, though unevenly, in the United States, each providing venues and opportunities for child education and development.

Bronfenbrenner would suggest that each of these venues could provide useful experiences to advance the development of a child of four. It is also true that there are encouragements of education and developmental advancements on each level, and differences between levels (*Microsystem, Mesosystem, Exosystem, and Macrosystem*). Educators should understand the links between institutions concerning age-related matters, and the implications that these linkages might have for the developing needs of children. Plans for classroom learning should take these levels of experience into account.

The first level is the *Microsystem*. This level provides opportunities for interactions in environments like home, siblings, parents and family. Bronfenbrenner's next outer level is the *Mesosystem*. This includes interactive opportunities with schools, churches, child-care centers, and neighborhoods. The next outer level is the *Exosystem*. In this area, children might have opportunities to visit their parents' workplace, interact with images and ideas from public media, and remain a source of responsibility for school boards and other community agencies. Finally, Bronfenbrenner identifies the *Macrosystem* as the gateway to larger society. This includes the shared values, beliefs, and ideas that can be shared with peers and others in social institutions (Bronfenbrenner, 1979).

Bronfenbrenner emphasized that the ecological model provided researchers with a perspective that enabled investigations of the immediate environments that happened to be available to developing children at any given time. For example, the child's emerging values and beliefs while attending age-related institutions like a school and a child-care center, and early encounters with peers, could be identified and isolated for study (Bronfenbrenner, 1986).

James Mark Baldwin (1861–1934) is often overlooked when there are discussions of major theorists who pinpoint *sociocultural* influences on human development and learning. Baldwin can also be classified among stage theorists such as Freud, Erikson, Piaget, and Vygotsky. Baldwin's argument reintroduces the age-old conundrum of *nature vs. nurture.*

During the early 1900s, when the field of psychology was impressed with learning theories inspired by behaviorism and classical conditioning, Baldwin proposed that development was not controlled by nature or nurture. Neither the learner nor the environment, according to Baldwin, has any practical influence on development. In his view, major influences on development come from environmental effects *on* human growth and development. In other words, it is through imitating the behaviors of others and subsequent interactions that development occurs. He viewed development and learning as an interactive process where developing children were influenced by social interactions, and the reverse is also true; children influence their environment (Baldwin, 1897).

Urie Bronfenbrenner, along a track similar to one that Vygotsky and Bandura traced, introduced a theory of human ecology. This approach to human development and learning conceptualized by Baldwin, Bandura, Bronfenbrenner, and Vygotsky is socioculturally based.

These theorists devoted major portions of their adult lives to discovering learning and development advances for individuals from birth through adulthood. Some have proposed that it occurs in incremental measures for all humans. Their theories take us in different directions, sometimes because of an individual's experiences, learner variations in will and motivation, and the child's capacity to understand objects and events during his or her lifetime of experiences. For educators, knowledge of their discoveries will contribute to an understanding of the nature and needs of learners.

3

Assessment in Early Development

The claim that we have learned how to measure hereditary intelligence has no scientific foundation. We cannot measure intelligence when we have never defined it, and we cannot speak of its hereditary basis after it has been indistinguishably fused with a thousand educational and environmental influences from the time of conception to the school age.

—Walter Lippmann

Assessments of programs, institutions, and individuals remain popular in the United States. Of these three areas of measurement, individual performance appears to be the most popular. There are a variety of assessments that are used to investigate normalcy, behavior, and other human qualities in infancy. Some testing, like intelligence, for example, is practically impossible to assess with high accuracy during infancy. However, many studies have tried to do so. In some test designs, responses to an imposed stimulus is observed and recorded, and values have been ascribed to the behavior (Fagan and McGrath, 1981).

There are a variety of infant assessments that have proven useful. Attachment behavior, for example, is an infant/caregiver reciprocal behavior. It is suggested by learning theorists that mothers have inherited basic caregiving responses that are stimulated in the presence of infants (Cairns, 1979). In 1969, John Bolby developed an ethological theory of attachment. Bolby suggested that it was not inherited characteristics that encouraged mother/infant attachment but rather mutual attraction through physical appearance and behavior.

In building this relationship, an attachment can be formed between the infant and caregiver. During infancy, a primary caregiver is essential. The attachment behavior that follows is not determined solely by the infant or the

73

caregiver. This interactive process can set the stage for reciprocal responses from caregiver and/or infant. For example, when a baby is frequently irritable and fussy a caregiver might not be as responsive as when the infant does not demonstrate fussiness. However, when caregivers are nonresponsive to the infant's persistent fussiness, a cycle of infant fussiness and irritability is likely to develop (Belsky, Rovine, and Taylor, 1984).

Ainsworth, through her extensive work with African infants, surmised that all infants are attached to their parents. She cited the ways in which an infant feels comfort in the presence of a caregiver as the *quality of the attachment* (Ainsworth, Blehar, Waters, and Wall, 1978).

Ainsworth and Bell (1970) developed an infant assessment test, *the Ainsworth Strange Situation Test.* In this assessment, infants and caregivers were observed in an unfamiliar environment and recorded in eight episodes identified as follows:

Episode 1. Infant and caregiver are brought to the observation room by the observer.
Episode 2. Infant and caregiver play together for several minutes.
Episode 3. Infant and caregiver play together with an unfamiliar adult.
Episode 4. Caregiver leaves the baby with the unfamiliar adult for three minutes.
Episode 5. The unfamiliar adult leaves and the caregiver returns.
Episode 6. The caregiver leaves the baby alone.
Episode 7. The stranger returns without the caregiver.
Episode 8. The stranger leaves, and the caregiver is reunited with her baby.

If the infant is *securely attached,* she will seek comfort from the caregiver in episode 8.

Secure attachment is observed when the infant shows interest in the stranger and shows interest in the strange setting, but will return to the caregiver's side for security.

Insecurely attached, resistant qualities demonstrated by the infant can be observed when the infant shows discomfort in the caregiver's absence from the scene. Insecurely attached avoidant infants will appear upset when left with an unfamiliar adult or in a strange setting. During episode 8, infants might resist being comforted and squirm or turn away from the caregiver. These behavioral classifications have been examined, and determined to last over time (Waters, 1983).

The most contentious activity in this domain is the frequent testing that is taking place because of requirements in the No Child Left Behind legislation.

Historically, our interest in the assessment of school children started with Alfred Binet in France. In 1905, Binet was appointed by the minister of education to develop a test that could measure mental capacity so as to identify school children who might benefit from special education. Within a few years, psychologists were testing children prior to school admission to sort them according to their "mental age" and reporting a score that has been labeled "IQ."

Binet's original test trials employed modest informal assessments of schoolchildren who appeared unwilling or unable to understand simple daily rituals. Binet arranged face-to-face individual meetings with referred children. Upon meeting he would offer to shake the child's hand. If the child complied, this meant a successful completion of the first skill. Binet would progress to simple questions like name, age, and home address. The number of completed answers would constitute the child's score.

Referred children were those with severe performance challenges, and Binet was aware that these preliminary assessments of their needs would not satisfy France's minister of education. This approach, however, could satisfy some preliminary questions helpful in satisfying an orientation to laboratory work and a final measuring instrument. Jean Piaget, as a recent Ph.D. graduate, worked in one of the explorative laboratories in France that assisted in developing Binet's intelligence tests. This discussion is continued in other parts of this book.

Today, testing is still popular, and sometimes required, for student admission to *gifted classes* as well as for placement in classes for the mentally challenged, and this is required by law. Limitations of IQ assessments have been identified by many in the field.

> The measurement of IQ is based on a series of assumptions that must be reviewed. First, the criterion for intellectual behavior is school performance. Thus the task and materials are designed around the materials used in school. This design would be of little concern if all that was of interest was, in fact, school performance. Unfortunately, the discussion has not been stopped at this point, but theorists have chosen instead to generalize test performance to all mental activity, not just performance. (Lewis, 1983, p. 10)

According to Lewis, our present IQ measures are in reality measures of school performance. The ability to perform successfully in school was the original mission of Binet in the original concept. When brought to the United States, the assumed capability of the new Stanford-Binet intelligence test changed and was used to rank thousands of citizen groups wherever they could be found.

In the early 1900s, when IQ tests were honored and used in many different venues, like schools, the military, the ranking for membership in academic organizations, and admission to university studies, IQ was accepted as a fixed birthright quantity and was generally assumed to be unaffected by opportunity (Wellman, 1932).

Intelligence has been promoted as a highly desirable label, meaning the more you have the better you are. When the word *intelligence* is noted in public media, more often than not the reference actually means *knowledge*. Marketers have also used intelligence as a label to imply desirable traits (multiple intelligence, emotional intelligence, learning styles, etc.), and have sold lots of trinkets to schools and parents on the strength of a poor understanding of the word by purchasers.

Intelligence in the general population has come to mean *knowledge* instead of designating its true meaning: *the capacity to acquire knowledge.* Today, erroneously, these words are used interchangeably. Intelligence since 1905 has meant that one has a high, moderate, or low capacity for acquiring knowledge, not *how much.*

A person could be highly intelligent but only moderately knowledgeable in a particular subject area. In the absence of experience, a learner would have no opportunity to acquire highly rated knowledge, even if the individual had an effective capacity to acquire that knowledge. Experience and opportunity frame the foundation of Lev Vygotsky's theory of the *zone of proximal development* that is discussed in other parts of this text.

Here it is theorized that a person with a high IQ would learn more, possibly at a faster rate, than one with a lower IQ, assuming for example that all members of a group have had equal experiences. If given time and individualized experiences rich with what is to be learned, the capacity for acquiring knowledge could be equal for most learners. This is an intention of individualized teaching and learning.

Individuals are not born with a fixed intelligence. The quality of experiences during the first 24 months of child rearing and the interaction between caregiver and child are significant factors in intellectual development for later years.

From the early 1900s until the mid-1960s, there were few disbelievers in the concept of a fixed intelligence. Beginning in the 1960s, however, the work of Hunt (1961), Kamin (1974), Hechinger (1979), and Hacker (1994) shed doubt on the idea that intelligence was fixed at birth. This idea was significant because of two problems: One was poor science, and the other was racism. Today, the idea of a fixed intelligence is practically extinct.

RACE AND THE POLITICS OF IQ

In the early 1900s, African Americans had few rights in the United States that were respected; racist practices existed in all walks of life yet were not thought of as problems. White groups primarily from Southern Europe were also subjects of intellectual derision, and occasionally Blacks were included statistically in these groups for good measure.

In the early 1900s Terman proposed that all children entering school for the first time should be tested and placed in classrooms according to their IQ score. Terman assisted in a crusade to separate Northern European children and their descendants from immigrants from Southern Europe and others whom he considered undesirable (Kamin, 1974).

In the group of "undesirables" were the almost 800,000 Irish who came to the United States in the 1840s to escape a famine. Aside from being poor, they were negatively valued for other reasons. Often having an ill-fitting, homemade appearance in clothing usually sewn by hand, they were mainly Roman Catholics in a land previously occupied by Protestants, who had arrived years earlier in their effort to escape religious persecution in their home country. The Protestant Irish-Americans were fearful that an overwhelming number of Catholics would acquire more power and influence in a land of opportunity than themselves.

At about that time in Germany, a large part of the population was pressing for reform. Conflicts led to a mass exodus to other countries; chief among them was the United States. Several students of Friedrich Froebel's were in these various groups that came to the United States. Caroline Frankenberger, one of Froebel's students, settled in Columbus, Ohio. She opened a kindergarten but returned to Germany when it was not successful.

Margarethe Schurz, another German immigrant, settled in Wisconsin and opened a kindergarten that was successful primarily because she moved into an area with a large number of German families who had settled there years earlier. Schurz is credited with opening the first successful German-language kindergarten in the United States.

Unlike Irish and Italian immigrants, Germans frequently came with wealth. They established German-speaking schools, and came to the United States seeking political freedom as well as economic opportunities. Large settlements in Columbus, Ohio, and Philadelphia led citizens to label these areas "Germantowns," and they exist today.

Native Americans

Under modest pressure from various human-rights activist groups in the United States like the transcendentalists and The Anti Slavery League, the U.S. Supreme Court ruled in favor of Native American rights to own property in Georgia that had belonged to them and their ancestors for centuries. At the same time, the Court denied Indians the use of their property for trade, barter, or sale to anyone other than the U.S. government.

Despite that Supreme Court ruling, in 1830, the U.S. Congress passed the *Indian Removal Act* and ordered the removal of five Native American tribes from land they owned in Georgia, to West of the Mississippi River because Whites wanted their land. The Cherokee nation took their case to the Supreme Court and won the right to own their land, where they had a long history of a settled community with governing bodies, community organizations, a newspaper, and schools.

In general, however, the white extermination of Native Americans and the enslavement of African Americans continued (Bernal, 1987).

In this act of relocation, Native Americans were forced to march hundreds of miles across country in severe winter weather. The deaths of women, children, and the elderly remain as a document of history. This deadly march was named the *Trail of Tears* (Harvey, Harjo, and Jackson, 1997).

Mexican Americans

In the West, Texas won its independence from Mexico in 1835, and that led to a treaty in 1848. Arizona, California, Nevada, Utah, Wyoming, and sections of New Mexico were transferred to the United States by Mexico (Murguia, 1975).

In the transfer, Mexican citizens were granted rights to move into Mexico or remain in the United States. Through manipulations, however, Mexicans who decided to remain in the newly ceded areas eventually lost their property rights to U.S. interests and like the Italians and Irish were viewed as undesirables (Weber, 1973).

In 1931, during the administration of President Herbert Hoover, a federal enactment of Mexican repatriation expelled up to 1.2 million U.S. citizens of Mexican ancestry from their homes in California and transported them out of the United States into Mexico (Balderrama and Rodriquez, 1995).

Born in the United States, many had never visited or lived in Mexico. It was the time of the Great Depression when these U.S. citizens were stripped of their basic civil liberties and transported out of their country to make way for "real Americans" who could then inherit the jobs that they left behind (Hecht, 2005).

American children of Mexican descent of that era experienced emotional trauma because they were forced to grow up in a Mexican society that rejected them as "anglicized," referring to them as "Nortenos."

IQ AND PUBLIC SCHOOLS

It should not be surprising that in the national social atmosphere of the early 1900s Terman's first report on the intellectual capacity of school children ranked immigrant children from Germany and other Northern European countries high and children in families from Southern Europe, Hispanics, Native Americans, and African Americans modest by comparison, as seen in Table 3.1 (Wickett, 2000). As Terman commented early in his report:

> It is interesting to note . . . the level of intelligence which is very, very common among Spanish-Indian and Mexican families of the Southwest and also among Negroes. Their dullness seems to be racial, or at least inherent in the family stocks from which they come. The fact that one meets this type with such extraordinary frequency among Indians, Mexicans, and Negroes suggests quite forcibly that the whole question of racial differences in mental traits will have to be taken up anew and by experimental methods. (Terman, 1919, pp. 91–92)

Table 3.1.   Terman's Measured Intelligence of School Children

Race	Number	Median IQ
Spanish	37	78
Portuguese	23	84
Italian	25	84
North European	14	105
American	49	106

Source: From L. M. Terman, *The intelligence of school children* (Boston: Houghton Mifflin, 1919), 56.

Studies reported in the 1970s suggested that family income could have a significant influence on mental test scores of preschool children (Willerman, Broman, and Fiedler, 1970). Terman's work of more than 80 years ago could be a measure of the effects of family *income* rather than the child's capacity to learn.

With more than 3,000 infants in their sample, the effects of family income and other socioeconomic indices on infant development were studied. Test scores were taken at eight months and at four years of age. Children with low mental scores at eight months who lived in low socioeconomic-status families *scored low* on the mental test at four years of age. Children with low mental scores at eight months who lived in families of high socioeconomic status achieved *above average* mental scores at four years of age (Willerman, et al. 1970).

In a more recent study, Liaw, Meisels, and Brooks-Gunn (1995) measured the effects of "active experiences" introduced through a planned intervention program for infant development. The study reported that active experiences in the home and at a family center were associated with higher IQ scores at ages one, two, and three. This evidence would lead a prudent person (to coin a phrase from Leon Kamin) to conclude that IQ scores are changeable, not fixed.

In the 1970s Hispanic and Black parents started to notice that an overwhelming number of their schoolchildren were being placed in remedial classes. The disproportionate placement of Black and Hispanic children in remedial classrooms became the focus of a national trend and brought attention to schools in major cities. Through support from the National Association for the Advancement of Colored People Legal Defense Fund and a public-interest law firm, six Black parents sued the California school system in state court. California authorities cited an inheritance of inferior genes, not racism, as the primary cause of remedial placements for this Black and Hispanic group of students.

In early court briefs, the defense for the state of California cited that one of the factors for lower intelligence scores by the students in the remedial classes was "a poorer genetic pool for all races ghettoized in the inner city." (*New York Times,* October 12, 1977, p. A20)

Finally, by the 1970s it became known that scientific studies reporting inferior IQ scores of Blacks when compared to IQ scores of Whites were found to be fraudulent (Rensberger, 1976; Hechinger, 1979).

The classic reports of the late Cyrl Burt, the eminent British psychologist whose research had long been accepted by many as evidence that differences in intelligence were hereditary, are now widely considered to be without scientific value. Because Dr. Burt's writings had been a major buttress of the view that Blacks have inherited inferior brains, his discrediting is regarded as a significant blow to the school of thought espoused by such persons as Arthur Jensen of the University of California, Richard Herrnstein of Harvard and William Shockley of Stanford.

Dr. Burt's research, unquestioned and highly influential before his death in 1971, has been criticized in psychological circles since 1972, when it was found to contain a number of impossibilities. (Rensberger, 1976, p. 9)

For some time now, testing and assessment have been a significant area of interest in schooling. In early childhood, assessment starts at birth and extends through all grades. However, assessments concerning neonatal development and general health are more often than not conducted in hospital environments by pediatricians.

Deficits and achievements in infant development are measured by neurologists, pediatricians, and psychologists. From observations of infants, neurologists measure cerebral DNA and estimate cell quantity and the effects of the absence of prenatal care and adequate nutrition. Psychologists observe an infant's expressions and related behaviors along with responses to specifically designed tasks. During the first 12 months, developmental changes are occurring rapidly and are difficult to measure.

There are also long-term studies during which infants are observed in families and social scientists record selected interactions between a child and his or her environment. Here, maternal and caregiver behaviors are commonly observed. Maternal care, however, can be overdemanding or depriving. This variability creates an interest in long-term infant/parent observations (Ainsworth, 1962; Niemeyer, 2002).

In the first year, with adequate nutrition, infant body weight normally increases threefold, but the weight gain for the brain is greater than in any other somatic area. This produces great changes in cognitive development because of a rapid increase in cell size, the number of dendrites, and the weight of the brain. Psychologists can observe the infant's reaction to the environment. For example, a few months after birth infants think that when a toy falls out of sight it no longer exists. However, a few months later the infant's eyes will try to locate an object that has fallen out of sight (Piaget, 1952).

Arnold Gesell, a psychologist and pediatrician, is among the earliest pioneers of infant testing (Gesell and Amatruda, 1941). Infant tests that were subsequently developed by others include a selection of items borrowed from the work of Gesell. His studies have also been expanded and revised by others (Knobloch and Pasamanick, 1974; Knobloch, Stevens, and Malone, 1980).

The most useful assessments have been developed to measure attention span, social participation, capacity for eliciting responses, and reflexive responses, in infants aged six months and younger. The most well-known neonatal tests are the *Graham/Rosenblith Behavioral Examination of Neonates* (Rosenblith, 1961), the *Prechtl Neurological Examination* (Prechtl and Beintema, 1964), and the *Neonatal Behavioral Assessment Scale* (Brazelton, 1973).

EMPIRICAL ASSESSMENTS OF INFANT REFLEXES

Reflexes govern a newborn's automatic movements. Reflexes are reactions to events in the environment, frequently beyond the infant's control. Those who study infant development are familiar with reflexes and how they can be observed. Listed in table 3.2 are common infant reflexes that follow birth.

Considerable attention has been focused on social skills demonstrated by infants and a comparison of periods during which they *select* a target and *attend*. This can encourage investigator interests away from reporting on intelligence, toward a notion of general skills as predictors of future cognitive development (Fagan and McGrath, 1981).

Developmental stages reported from the work of Jean Piaget have become popular and difficult to ignore in the literature. A significant number of infant

Table 3.2.   Infant Reflexes Subject to Assessment

Reflex:	blinking eyes
Stimulation:	puff of air or blinking light
Infant Response:	close both eyes
Reflex:	Babinski
Stimulation:	stroke sole of foot
Infant Response:	twist foot in, fan toes out
Reflex:	grasping
Stimulation:	palms touch
Infant Response:	tight grasp
Reflex:	Moro
Stimulation:	sudden loud noise or loss of support
Infant Response:	arches back, throws head back, stretches arms and legs
Reflex:	rooting
Stimulation:	stroke cheek
Infant Response:	opens mouth, starts suckling
Reflex:	stepping
Stimulation:	lowers feet to touch surface
Infant Response:	moves feet as if to walk
Reflex:	sucking
Stimulation:	object touching mouth
Infant Response:	sucks automatically
Reflex:	swimming
Stimulation:	placed face-down in water
Infant Response:	makes swimming movements
Reflex:	tonic neck
Stimulation:	placed on back
Infant Response:	forms fist with both hands, turns head to right

studies have focused on Piaget's sensorimotor stage of development. This is true because in part, "average" behaviors for this stage are clearly articulated and relatively easy to measure (Beilin, 1992).

Scales of infant development derived from Piaget's original observations were constructed by Uzgiris and Hunt (1975). Using these scales, 84 infants ranging in age from one to 24 months were examined. The first scale, consisting of 14 steps, evaluates the infant's *visual pursuit* and *object permanence.* A comparison is made between the infant's performance and the extent to which that performance compares with Piaget's *object permanence* category. The second scale has 13 steps and examines the means by which the subject obtains desired results. An additional scale has nine steps and examines vocal (nine steps) and gesture (nine steps) imitations (Uzgiris and Hunt, 1975; Dunst, 1980).

Once children are in school, there are group assessments that report their academic progress and psychological status. Occasionally, individual assessments will lead to a special placement for a child. For a child to be placed in a class for the academically and/or the physically challenged, however, an individual assessment of the specific area(s) of concern must be evaluated by a psychologist certified in the field of testing.

4

How We Know

I went to the woods because I wished to live deliberately, to front only the
essential facts of life; and see if I could not learn what it had to teach.

—Henry David Thoreau

In today's early-childhood environments children are pressed to perform academic tasks that are predisposed to memorization of factual material. Factual data can have an important role in knowledge acquisition, but facts presented in rote fashion do not constitute the primary features of *how young
children should be taught*. Such restrictive approaches seldom embody what
is commonly needed to support comprehensive knowledge acquisition for
early childhood learners (Reeder, 2005).

Memory traces that are limited to isolated bits of factual matter (like mem-
orizing a multiplication table, for example) can isolate factual competence
from overall meanings that mathematical principles require in our daily
lives. For example, music is often eliminated from the early-childhood curriculum to make place for extended math and word memory drill. Education
planners making such changes appear unaware that music is based on *mathematical foundations*, and words in song are directly related to words in *myr-
iad contexts*.

Drill and test pedagogies are being introduced in early-childhood education
by planners whose academic training was earned in *elementary education,*
where principles of what *should be taught* is a primary goal, rather than em-
bracing the early child principles of understanding *how children learn* (Weber, 1984).

More often than not, these requirements are imposed by state education agencies in response to institutional demands, presented as the "will of the public," for school improvement. The so-called improvements are aimed at raising the scores of school children on state and national tests designed to measure what children have been taught, and what the agencies hope they know. To this audience, educational goals can best be achieved though drill, rote memory, and persistent paper-and-pencil work.

As children expand their competencies beyond Piaget's stage of *concrete operations* and Erikson's stage of achieved *industry,* narrow concepts in computational mathematics, with rote memory and drill, can advance knowledge in a limited context and enable children to acquire some basic skills concepts, like how to count money and make change. In the overall picture of *understanding mathematics,* such approaches are too limited to enable a comprehensive understanding of mathematics (Reeder, 2005).

A full understanding of mathematics comes from early-childhood traditions in curricula where learners are exposed to blocks and small shapes are manipulated in an interactive process while exploring and examining similarities and differences. The articulation of related qualities should be encouraged between children in small groups as they engage in the discovery of time, spatial relationships, and scale. These concepts are integrated with what they have learned from previous experiences in family, community, and other social environments (Laurendeau and Pinard, 1970; Liben, Moore, and Golbeck, 1982; Somerville and Bryant, 1985).

A curriculum in arithmetic and mathematics for children in early-childhood classrooms (pre-K–4) is significantly different from that found in elementary grades (4–6) (Kamii, 1976, 1989; Kamii and DeClark, 1985).

Since at least the mid-80s, findings have accumulated from research investigating the nature of misunderstanding. The research reveals unequivocally that the ability to memorize facts does not necessarily imply understanding of a concept. Apparently, understanding is not so much a destination as it is a point along a continuum. We may never arrive at perfect understanding of a subject, but we can deepen our understanding beyond the superficial. At some point, learners' grasp of the concept becomes deep or sophisticated enough that they can use their knowledge in a practical way. It is this level of comprehension that teachers aim for, that we qualify as understanding something. That is, "understanding" can be defined as the ability to apply a new concept in a non-textbook or classroom context; use a concept to make sense of complex, real-world situations; or express a concept in a meaningful way to others. (Reeder, 2005)

In the following discussion, it will be interesting to note that traces of information are integrated through our *experience, attention,* and *perception,* not isolated in any single area. Therefore, bits of information are best retrieved when presented to the learner in *context* and not in *isolation.* When presented in isolation, learners must possess the additional skill to integrate various isolated chunks of meanings on their own.

All children learn a great deal *before* attending school. By the first day of formal schooling, children have mastered the language of parents and siblings. They have also learned the names of their favorite sports figures, media heroes, foods, neighbors, and TV personalities; days of the week; names and general meanings of holidays, and much more. Low test scores achieved by some children seldom indicate the total of what they know and seldom what they are *capable of learning.*

All people learn through the same human process regardless of ethnicity or gender. What we all learn is derived from *experience.* Experience is everything that we encounter during our waking hours. When we *attend* to these *experiences,* traces of objects and events enter our memory and in short order become *learned.* When today's educators speak about *learning,* especially the extent to which a student has *learned a concept or idea,* more often than not they are referring to *performance.* All individuals, regardless of age, skin color, gender, or income, *learn the same way.* There are significant differences in *experiences* to which we are exposed, as well as differences in whether we decide to *attend* to an *experience,* and what we might *perceive* as a result of attending to an experience. Experience and attending are significant parts of the knowledge-acquisition process but do not constitute the whole of *learning* (Morgan, 2003; Brodal, 1998; Powers, 1973).

The acquisition of knowledge follows several steps and stages that include *experience, attention, perception, short-term memory,* and *long-term memory*—in that order. Our teachers, test examiners, friends, and other audiences can demonstrate what has been learned by *retrieving* previously acquired knowledge from memory. *Retrieval* is at work when we are taking a written test, speaking to an audience, or performing a laboratory experiment. And, despite its immediacy, even that up-to-the-minute retrieval during a conversation is an *experience* from which additional learning can occur (Morgan, 2003).

Experiences differ. Children growing up in communities with social realities associated with low family income, moderately educated parents, and sometimes negative attitudes of others toward them will start school having acquired a great deal of useful knowledge from a set of experiences shaped primarily by their domestic circumstances.

For some, what is learned from these experiences will be useful as they perform academic tasks, yet for other children (especially those from families of modest income), their common family and neighborhood experiences will seldom be rewarded in their classrooms because such knowledge is incompatible with schoolwork. Children from low-income families will acquire knowledge that is useful and sometimes essential in their home and community, but this same knowledge will seldom be considered academically valuable (Bernstein, 1961).

So *being able to learn* is not a problem here; however, many educators are more concerned about *what* students can retrieve from memory during a testing situation. Children who are unable to perform under such circumstances are often labeled "challenged learners." Educators have determined in advance what school children should know. What children should know has been identified at the level of the state education department, integrated into the curriculum. This "should-know" knowledge frames the questions selected for standardized tests that all school children are required to successfully complete. Some school districts have made successful retrieval of correct answers from tests a mandatory step before a student can advance to the next grade. Such tests have been called "high stakes." This process has become essential for some school districts since the inauguration of the No Child Left Behind Act.

WHAT IS LEARNING?

Learning is a biological/chemical process that creates knowledge through our central nervous system (CNS; spinal cord and the brain). Acquired knowledge is stored in the brain (memory). The brain and spinal cord (CNS) are located in dark chambers of our body with no access to the outside world. The brain is provided access to our world of experiences through our senses: visual, auditory, tactile, olfactory, and taste (Brodal, 1998).

The senses are challenged in different ways by our *experiences.* Some *experiences* occur informally, like a birthday party or a parade, for example, while others are formal, like a child's exposure to a teacher's planned lesson in a classroom. Great variations of other exposures are limited only by a person's imagination.

Learners, consciously and/or subconsciously, decide whether or not to *attend* to an experience. Information to which one does not attend will probably not be *learned* because it will not have access to the remaining stages in the process. So the first step in learning is *experience,* and the next stage is *attending (attention).* These stages are followed by perception, *short-term memory, long-term memory,* and *retrieval.* These steps and stages do not have an objective location in the human body. In essence, they serve as a metaphor for information processing by the human organism.

Information from an *experience* that captures our *attention* is selected through *perception,* and this information will be captured by our *short-term memory* and passed along to our *long-term memory*. We now know that knowledge in long-term memory is stored in the brain and, once there, is considered *what is known by the individual*. If you are in school, a frequent request for *retrieval* (oral queries, written tests, etc.) will be required for academic performance to prove what you have learned.

Our brain consists of layers and rounded structures designed to carry out a series of complex functions involving networks requiring large numbers of *neurons*. Information is carried from an experience to the brain through the CNS, a system of communication and control (Brodal, 1998).

Th human nervous system is built upon the *neuron* as its primary structure for transmitting and receiving information. The *neuron* is composed of a cell body and its extensions. Found on all sides of the nerve cell are thin microscopic dendrites that carry impulses *toward* the cell body. The *axon* is a thick extension that carries information *away* from the cell body. Millions of neurons exist in the human system of knowledge acquisition.

The end of each axon is close to a dendrite of an adjoining neuron, but they do not touch. A microscopic gap is maintained between the *axon* of one neuron and the *dendrite* of the next neuron. This gap is called the *synapse*. The gap between the *axon* of one cell and *dendrite* of an adjoining cell is small enough to allow chemical signals (*neurotransmissions)* to pass between them. A neurotransmitter is the substance released at the nerve endings when an impulse is transmitted to a neuron, gland, or muscle.

Healthy nerve cells contain an equal number of positively or negatively charged ions. The movement of impulses through the nerve cells calls for chemical and electrical changes. Prior to the transmission of impulses, the outside layers of the nerve cell are composed of electrically charged positive sodium *ions*. Its inside layer is composed of electrically charged negative potassium *ions*. When the neuron is transmitting, the outside of the neuron becomes *negative,* and the inside becomes *positive*. As soon as the impulse passes, the sodium and potassium ions return to their original state. When a neuron transmits an impulse, similar changes occur in all parts of the cell.

In a healthy CNS, information sent from different sensory neurons is the same. Information sent from a taste sensation on the tongue is chemically identical to the information transmitted from a touch on the tip of a finger, but the information is received and processed in different areas of the brain. In this example, impulses are identified as different experiences—taste and touch. As the brain translates and identifies these sensations as different experiences, it sends impulses back to the stimulated areas through motor neurons. Muscles and glands are stimulated into action, and they will contract or secrete, in that order. This transmission of impulses from different sensory neurons to the brain, then to the motor neuron, is called a *reflex arc*. The reflex arc is the simplest reflex pattern found in the CNS.

5

Public Policy

States must improve their standards for prekindergarten education if programs are to produce the large gains in learning and development that the nation seeks. Teachers are required to have a BA and specialized training in preschool education in only 13 state preschool initiatives, whereas all public K–12 teachers must hold 4-year degrees and be state licensed or certified by the end of the 2005–2006 school year. States should apply high standards to all programs, so that no child can slip through the cracks.

—National Institute for Early Education Research

There are many in the field of preschool education who suggest that quality child care and preschool education are too costly to survive on a fee-for-service basis. They go on to suggest that to avoid the warehousing of children to enable women in poor families to work, these caretakers need higher salaries to afford the cost of adequate child care for their children, or that care for their children must be a matter of public policy. Currently, state and federal educational initiatives are moving in the direction of integrating child care with regular public education. Such integration would bring the quality of child care to the level of public schooling (Barnett, Hustedt, Robbin, & Schulman, 2004).

In the mid-1930s, families in the United States experienced the greatest surge of public policy initiatives in their country's history. Through the creation of a group of federal programs, poor families became eligible for Social Security and Aid to Families with Dependent Children (AFDC), sometimes referred to as "welfare." The Works Progress Administration (WPA) provided jobs for adult males, and the Civilian Conservation Corps provided employment for male teens in poor families. These programs also hired office personnel and related support services and thus provided employment for social workers, clerks, secretaries, administrators, educators, and various other professionals, most of whom were also among the unemployed because of the Great Depression.

Some programs that were started in the 1930s have been gradually phased out as the Great Depression waned, while others, like Social Security, still remain in various forms. Still fully implemented today are an embattled Social Security System and a severely modified and limited program similar to AFDC.

Social programs of the 1930s marked the emergence of a national philosophy that in part was used to justify federal initiatives. Some social programs were initiated because of challenging economic conditions that created a significant increase in poor families. These challenges were caused in large part by the collapse of the Wall Street financial markets and related depressing economic conditions affecting the entire nation.

Some economists were fearful that this depressing era marked the demise of capitalism. Families in the United States faced a critical cutback of satisfaction of basic human needs like food, clothing, and housing. During this period, young children in general and racial minorities in particular were among the most harshly victimized.

Public policy can take various forms, but it is often enacted through programs that are proposed and legislated through an interactive congressional process that culminates with funding of an approved initiative. This process travels a pathway that starts with recommendations, discussions, and deal making by elected and appointed officials at various levels of state and national government.

Public policy is an enactment of law that becomes a legal requirement culminating in allocation(s) of funds for programs intended to satisfy a public need. Later in this chapter, public policy in the 1990s leading to the funding of infant and toddler programs will be discussed.

Public policy programs and laws are often designed for the education, health, safety, and well-being of the general public or a segment of it. Some initiatives might also provide financial assistance directly to cities and towns to support libraries, museums, schools, parks, and recreation centers, for example. In 2005, such an initiative was voted for Louisiana, Mississippi, and Alabama, after the severe Katrina weather disaster.

RIGHTS VS. PRIVILEGES

Franklin Delano Roosevelt, a new U.S. president in 1933, took office after he defeated President Herbert Hoover, who is still remembered by older citizens as the president responsible for the Great Depression. Roosevelt's terms as president occurred during a time when more than 25 percent of the U.S. adult population was out of work.

Roosevelt introduced a philosophy of *public policy* intended to lift families out of their severe financial depression. This new national philosophy promoted the idea that the United States had an obligation to its citizens to insure a safe, healthy life for families when, through no fault of their own, national conditions made it impossible for them to provide for basic needs for themselves and their dependents.

This new attitude about public policy identified federal assistance to families, under certain circumstances, as a *right* and not a *privilege*. In addition to identifying federal assistance a public right, federal aid to benefit financially troubled families became recognized as essential public policy.

Through the 1920s, under the leadership of President Herbert Hoover, those responsible for enacting public policy viewed aid to poor families as a threat to their initiative to work. It was assumed by policy makers that a willingness to work among otherwise self-motivated adults would become unattractive if they received federal assistance. This assumption became a common mantra in the corporate community. The president, being close to the industrialists of his day, mirrored corporate fears that aid to the poor would undercut the availability of low-cost labor.

It is remarkable how many present-day entrepreneurs, who became wealthy and affluent through federal aid to themselves and their families, rail against the notion of federal assistance as a right for the impoverished today.

Legislated as AFDC, AFDC gradually became known as *public assistance* and/or *public welfare* for needy families. Though intended for the health and welfare of children in families, this aid was distributed to adults who were their primary caregivers. At the time of its inauguration, such assistance was thought to be temporary until families regained financial stability.

This public policy did become a way of life for a few. In the best of times, a consistent 20 percent of all children in the United States will grow up in poverty. Work opportunities for their parents are restricted by race, ethnicity, gender, and access to a quality education. As conditions of poverty became generational, this seemingly persistent carryover in poor families became known as the *cycle of poverty* (Zigler and Styfco, 1994).

The public appeared willing to accept the new 1930s philosophy of federal aid as a *right,* in part, because needy families of the 1930s and 1940s, who were frequently unemployed, were predominantly White. The public seemed unwilling to extend such *rights* to the "last to be hired, first to be fired" African Americans, Native Americans, and Hispanics.

Minorities experienced restrictions in employment, education, and commerce, through an enforcement of state and federal laws. The work of Martin Luther King and African American political activists was 25–30 years away. As the 1940s ushered in manufacturing jobs in preparation for WWII, Whites were once again employed in large numbers, but fewer minorities were hired during this period of well-paid employment. Minorities who were fortunate enough to be hired were assigned menial labor and consistently remained at the lowest salary levels. For the most part, minority adults and their families were left behind, and many turned to the public policy initiatives of President Roosevelt for help.

During the buildup for WWII, many Whites were employed, but too many minorities were not. President Roosevelt was destined to change this through the issuance of Executive Order 8802. The *policy* remained, but the *practice* changed, and a national social picture of family conditions emerged when aid to the poor returned to the pre-1930s national consciousness, which viewed federal assistance to poor families as a *privilege,* not a *right.*

Despite the reemergence of this conservative view, some aid to needy families in the United States, though uneven and inadequate, remained available to all poor families. In part, this was true because many White families also remained trapped in poverty.

In the 1940s, Bayard Rustin and A. Phillip Randolph, Black political activists, organized African American communities and threatened a march on Washington, D.C., to demonstrate against public policy regulations restricting employment opportunities based on race. To avoid demonstrations in the nation's capital, President Roosevelt issued Executive Order 8802 banning discrimination in hiring by firms receiving federal contracts. Demonstrations against racist public policies by African American citizens would be set aside until the emergence of demonstrations in the 1960s.

During the 1930s Great Depression, the WPA, through establishing nursery schools, provided services for preschool children during the same hours as public schools were opened to their older siblings. Unfortunately, the best that many such programs provided would be limited to custodial care. A purpose concurrent with child care was providing employment for poor women and daily care for their children, primarily to free them for wartime employment. This employment was also intended to reduce the ravages of the Great Depression on poor families (Hymes, 1978–1979).

WPA programs attracted a large number of new teachers of modest education and competence to the field of early-childhood education and thereby attracted a new group of activists to the field of early education.

In the 1940s the labor of women was sought to assist with the national war effort. To free women for national domestic needs, it was necessary to provide child care. This freeing of women to provide war-production labor was made possible by the Lanham Act (1941–1945). Serving over 500,000 children, the Lanham Act Child Care Programs of World War II provided support for neighborhood centers and staff to care for the children of working mothers. Parents were charged a nominal fee, and municipalities were required to provide support in the form of in-kind contributions. The preponderance of Lanham Centers (over 90 percent) were located in public schools.

In the early 1970s, university-based social scientists, in cooperation with their counterparts working in various federal agencies, identified poverty as a major problem in the United States and ultimately an embarrassment to a wealthy country. The persistence of poor families and the increase of children in poverty seemed to be more prevalent in particular areas of the country. Once identified, poverty also appeared persistent in particular families and communities. This led social scientists to identify some aspects of poverty as a "cycle." Breaking this cycle became the mission of national public policy initiatives.

While it was recognized that racism and sexism (single mothers) might highlight certain causative factors, it was thought that involving poor families in the planning and implementation of aid to families like themselves might be helpful in breaking this cycle.

In the wake of spiraling individual and family poverty, in 1965 the federal government initiated Head Start, a child-care program for poor families. Program guidelines identified a comprehensive approach to the child-care needs of the poor. Providing preschool education and improving nutrition, social services, dental services, and medical services for the poor were viewed as essential steps toward reducing the entanglement of families in the cycle of poverty (Berrueta-Clement, Schweinhart, Barnett, Epstein, & Weikart 1984; Pizzo, 1990).

Some thought that such cycles could be thwarted by improving the educational opportunities for the next generation of poor children. Also, through funding requirements that parents of children in the program must have membership and voting rights on Head Start community governing boards, families of moderate and low income were empowered. With these new powers granted to poor parents, few thought that Head Start would survive, since this placed them in a higher status than parent groups in public schools.

With these significant *social components* emerging, it was difficult for planners to maintain the image of Head Start as a *preschool educational program*, and not primarily *social engineering*. Despite the obvious identity conflicts over how preschool education is traditionally viewed, new initiatives granting power to parents were implemented by the Head Start originators (Leik and Chalkley, 1990).

Many ideas that influenced Head Start were borrowed from philosophies and practices of kindergartens and nursery schools from the early 1900s and comparable settlement-house programs for poor immigrant European families. Programs for immigrant families were first introduced by Jacob Riis and Jane Addams in the late 1800s and early 1900s to settlement houses in several major cities. Such programs demonstrated many social goals for poor, language-challenged immigrants. These programs included child care, free milk for children, voter rights education, the search for employment, and learning language for citizenship. Sometimes art and music classes were available.

In 2005, much to the surprise of the original social and educational planners, Project Head Start celebrated its 40th anniversary, and to some it remains the centerpiece of the *war on poverty* started in the 1960s and still needed today. Finally, there is a growing public belief that early childhood care and education should be a *right* in the same manner that kindergarten through the 12th grade is provided through public education. This needs to be done through an expansion of services for families. These services should assure flexible parental-leave policies, safe and affordable child-care services, and a thoughtful integration of education and care (Kamerman, 2005).

INFANTS, TODDLERS, AND PUBLIC POLICY

Infants, birth to 12 months, and toddlers, 12 to 24 months, are included under the title of infants and toddlers, but there are few federally supported services for these age groups. As of this writing, there are federally funded service and research programs for infants and toddlers of poor parents in modest proportions. Gradually, state-funded programs are emerging along with guidelines for the certification of teachers for this age group.

There are several reasons for a lingering interest in infant/toddler programs. One comes from the business world. Young employable adults willing to work for minimum wage often have infants and other young children. State and federal governments have expressed interest in providing child-care services as a means of freeing low-income adults for employment. Another reason rests with the general population. There is a persistent public and professional belief that government-funded programs for children in poor families can over time reduce the poverty rate. Theories that continue along these lines suggest that empowering academically competent young learners in poor families today can alter the persistent cycle of poverty by improving the lives of future families (Mallory and Goldsmith, 1990).

To support these ideas, it is noted that Project Head Start was inaugurated in the 1960s in many communities where kindergarten was neither provided nor expected, and studies have documented several cost-effective benefits to families of Head Start graduates.

In 1995, programs for infants and toddlers become a part of public policy initiatives extending national Head Start funding to younger recipients and expectant mothers in poor families. Legislative, theoretical, and philosophical support for federally funded infant/toddler programs comes from various sources. Some supporters suggest an expansion of the Head Start educational philosophy, while others support child care for poor parents so they might work or acquire education/training as preparation for employment.

In the latter idea, supporters argue, cost benefits would ultimately accrue by reducing single parents' need for welfare assistance. This is a variation on the right vs. privilege theorizing that has gradually reduced benefits through federal legislative action, as well as the length of time that adults can remain eligible for aid to dependent children.

In the United States local and state legislatures have enacted laws that require school attendance. Such bodies also establish age-attendance policies and policies establishing minimum teacher training and general eligibility for teacher certification. Some communities accept requirements established by the state, while others enact additional requirements of their own. State financial support of salaries for schoolteachers, administrators, and those who deliver associated services is available to certified personnel who work in schools and related facilities that children are required to attend.

As of this writing, public school attendance, though sometimes available, is not required of children three years old and younger. This creates a category of child-care worker whose salary is substantially lower than that of a certified teacher. This lower salary status can improve when the child-care worker can produce evidence of an educational attainment equal to minimum teacher-certification requirements. It is this group that must have federal- or state-sponsored child care (Head Start, Right Start, Early Head Start, etc.) for their own children to enable them to work for the modest wages generally paid to workers in today's proprietary, state, and federally sponsored child-care programs. As reported in a 2004 national report *State of Preschool:*

> The states vary greatly in how they pick up where the federal and private programs leave off. There is a wide gap between states like Oklahoma and Georgia, which make programs available for all four-year-olds, and states like Indiana, South Dakota, and Utah, which provide no state programs. In the middle states like Colorado, Iowa, Washington, programs are developed for at-risk and economically disadvantaged populations (Barnett et al., 2004).

Employees in child-care programs and their children can qualify for care are often members of an at-risk population. When employed in a minimum-wage child-care program, however, having two parent incomes in a household could render a family ineligible for state and federally sponsored placement for their own children. And their modest academic qualifications could make it difficult for them to advance their academic status.

Since the inception of Head Start in the mid-1960s, the requirements for Head Start teachers was gradually reduced from public school teacher certification to a minimum of high school completion, and salaries were reduced to minimum wage. In some states, adults without high school completion were hired as teachers in early-education centers.

In the early 1990s, Head Start teachers were required by federal mandate to obtain a two-year post–high school degree. Community-based technical schools grasped this as an opportunity to increase their student population and quickly developed two-year child-care programs. By the year 2000, Head Start teachers were required by federal mandate to acquire a four-year degree in Early Childhood Education or an equivalent. Higher salaries were offered as an attractive incentive.

One would surmise that teachers who had previously achieved a two-year degree would now be able to add an additional two years to satisfy new requirements for a four-year degree, but that was not the case. The AA degree that most of the Head Start teachers had earned to satisfy the earlier two-year requirement was earned at a technical college whose credits are not generally accepted at academic institutions as credit toward a four-year academic degree.

As of now, Head Start teachers with a two-year technical degree must start work toward a four-year academic degree at the same level as high school graduates and set aside their technical school AA degree. These predicaments, in which many of today's Head Start teachers find themselves, remain unresolved today.

States without mandated programs for children under the age of four have not contemplated such problems outside of Head Start, which is federally funded. Falling short of actually proposing certification requirements for teachers of infants and toddlers, many state education departments have left worker requirements to their social service divisions and not education departments. Minimum requirements are established by noneducation agencies, which establish rules for housing, food, safety, and the general care of infants and toddlers. Some state agencies, however, recommend and in some cases require high school completion or a two-year minimum completion of post–high school education to qualify as an infant/toddler caregiver. As of this writing, most candidates are attending technical colleges for these AA degrees.

Finally, an AA degree program in a technical college has many basic flaws when providing "training" in early-childhood education. One problem is the practice of recruiting "teachers" who work for modest salaries, who in turn train child-care workers who eventually work for minimum wage. This is excused by some who view services to children from birth to age two as "care" and not "education" (Table 3.1). The mission of many two-year technical college early-childhood courses are focused primarily on *credentialing* individuals for the purpose of "caring" for the young children of poor parents—not "educating" teachers. In these arrangements, benefits accrue to the economy in that poor parents are released for employment in local factories and neighborhood discount stores. The benefit for minimum-wage women who are child-care workers is medical insurance or them and their children.

Education policy in the states is controlled by a *Board of Regents* or similar policy-making bodies. State boards of regents or their academic counterparts influence education policy in all states, and it is unlikely that the need for educating children will take precedence over the needs of industry for educated, low-wage workers in the respective states.

EARLY HEAD START

In 1995, a small percentage of Head Start funds was allocated to an experimental program for at-risk infants and their parents. The 1994 reauthorization of Head Start stated that in 1995, 3 percent of the annual Head Start budget would be allocated to Early Head Start projects and this allocation would increase to 9 percent for 2001 and 10 percent by 2003. As of this writing, Early Head Start programs intervene in families through three-tiered services for low-income expectant mothers.

One tier encompasses home-based services, while the other two are center based, involving a unique mixed methods approach. These service tiers include home visits, health care, family support strategies, case management, and information concerning infant care and feeding as well as child growth and development seminars, including child-rearing practices. Early Head Start centers, an experimental federally funded program, provide infant/toddler out-of-home center care for children six months to two years of age. Programs are promoted as two-generational, while some programs are planned to retain infants through age three. Some have claimed that public policy has gone astray in the direction of services for young children because there is a proliferation of programs for this group. As of this writing, there are almost 70 federal programs within nine federal agencies that are designed to provide education, care, or both for children under five ("Early Education and Care," 2000).

Public policy has become a significant force in the expansion of infant and toddler community-based programs, and four-year universities have started to focus on this phenomenon. This is especially true for services that are designed for families with modest means. As of this writing, a few states and the federal government are the most active participants in the design of modern infant and toddler initiatives. It is also true that several state teacher certification agencies are in precertification phases of establishing professional standards for infant and toddler caregivers.

While participants in the planning and implementation of infant and toddler programs are proprietary and federal government sponsored, the preponderance of interest in programs for this age group is being investigated by state-based education agencies. Public policy initiatives improve the lives of all members of poor families through the implementation of early intervention programs for their children. Such programs also serve to enhance the future of family members of all ages, and ultimately change neighborhoods for the better.

In 1995, public policy in the United States introduced support for the early stages of an education system for infants. When completed in the near future, such public policy will provide a continuity of seamless educational opportunities for all children from birth through the 12th grade.

The public can expect that through an extension of the *No Child Left Behind* public policy, the future will eventually bring to the public an education system that starts at birth and ends in young adulthood. This new infant and toddler initiative intervened when a selected group of low-income families who were expecting a newborn were invited by newly hired Head Start family service workers to participate in an initial experimental phase of *Early Head Start.*

Early Head Start family service workers, utilizing home-based, center-based, and sometimes mixed methods, provided family-enriching activities and prebirth experiences for low-income pregnant women. Information was also provided for expectant mothers about their infants' growth and development after birth, and daily services were provided for their babies in two-year center-based programs that commenced when infants were six months of age.

In 2004 data were assembled to determine, among other things, how to establish effective daily programs for infants and toddlers. As of this writing, over 600 programs have been established, and communities are actively hiring infant/toddler professionals while recruiting pregnant women from low- and modest-income families for the next phase of participants (Barnett et al., 2004).

Schooling for children of all ages requires the involvement of parents and significant adults in the education of children. Early Head Start introduced expectant mothers to the learning capacity of their infants and established a belief among family members of the need for families to support the work of their school. As infant and toddler programs are made permanent, continuity in the education of children in the United States from birth through grade 12 will become a reality.

Public policy initiatives introduced the first Head Start programs during the summer in the mid-1960s.Within ten years this public policy initiative had been extended to include children in kindergarten and first and second grades. The intention here was to advance Head Start philosophy throughout the public school system. Head Start was active in communities where proposals were presented to federal agencies based upon neighborhood financial conditions. Pockets of poverty existed in various cities, and public policy initiatives funded Head Start because research in academic literature presented arguments that the number of depressed neighborhoods could be reduced with an infusion of health, social services, nutrition, and educational improvements. In addition, parents were written into the propositions as participants in policy matters. A critical role for parents in decision-making policy matters exists today.

Many have concluded that the Head Start policy of including a significant role for parents provided an impetus for change in traditional parent-teacher organizations, and encouraged a more active agenda that still exists today. Parent involvement in neighborhood-based Head Start policy is thought to have created a new impetus for home schooling. That interest has expanded a commercial market of attractive materials for parent-directed activities to use with their infants and toddlers. These kits, books, and curricula are available commercially and are accompanied with instructions for implementation.

Encouragement and advice that accompany materials for home schoolers should not be used as a step-by-step set of instructions. Human diversity is vast, and it would be impossible for authors and service providers to design perfectly scripted how-to measures that are characteristic of all learners. Such uses could lead to parental assumptions of failure when their child's behavior does not match with precision what is described in the text.

Teachers, school authorities, and educational planners encourage parent participation in the work of the school. Today, all Head Start proposals must have an approving signature from the Head Start neighborhood parents' advisory board, and the number of children being home schooled is increasing.

Why initiate a public policy for Early Head Start? Why infant and toddler literacy intervention? In the past few years, international academic test performance of children from developed countries suggested that fourth-grade children in the United States were equal to children in other countries like ours. This is not true for U.S. children in higher grades, however.

For educators, this suggests that early attention to teaching and learning can reap exceptional benefits for our young, but such gains can also decline in later years (Barnouw, 1970). Often, parents are willing to acknowledge the benefits of preschool, including infant and toddler programs. Their concern is expressed in a variety of ways but tends to generalize around their belief that giving up their child's daytime learning to institutional care is too much of a sacrifice because it places the acquisition of religious and social values by their children in the hands of adults other than themselves. Infant and toddler programs that are provided to low-income parents through federal funding, however, hear fewer of these concerns.

There is a long history of public policy interventions designed to improve family life through social and educational services. There is a similar history of neighborhood-based nursery schools that grew without public policy initiatives. By 1930, according to the U.S. Office of Education, there were 262 active nursery schools without federal funds. By 1935, there were almost 2,000 nursery schools serving 75,000 children (Hymes, 1978–1979).

Christine Heinig, a longtime activist in the nursery-school movement, discussed the emergency nursery schools and the wartime child-care centers that existed through public policy initiatives from 1933 through 1946:

> The focus was not on unemployed nursery school teachers but on teachers in general. Communities, hard pressed financially, had cut out every teaching job that could be eliminated: art, music, Latin, home economics, physical education. . . . There were thousands of unemployed teachers, cooks, and custodians. Providing employment was a great need. Employment wasn't the only goal, however. The benefits to children were also stressed in the first announcement by Harry Hopkins. The nursery schools were charged, and this is another quotation: . . . with combating the physical and mental handicaps being imposed upon young children by conditions incident to our current economic and social difficulties. (Hymes, 1978–1979, p. 9)

Starting with a mother's period of birth expectancy, it is important for parents to start reading about development and learning of their children after birth. This includes a search and review of children's literature that can be considered appropriate for the interest and joy of their children (Chall, 2000; Acredolo and Goodwin, 1998).

This also includes a willingness of parents to share in the care, development, and safety of their children with well-trained professionals. Parents should visit child-care centers and observe their level of quality with other parents who use such services prior to enrolling their own children.

Parents should also start thinking about literacy and gathering read-to books during the mother's pregnancy, thereby having a selection of reading materials in hand at birth. Reading to infants cannot start too early. Early involvement will set the stage for a lifelong relationship between parents and children (Chall, 1990; Beaty, 2005).

Infant/toddler programs for low-income families that were inaugurated in 1995 through federal funding were designed specifically to include education and support for parenting, family development (including social services), and child development from birth through the remainder of Head Start, a pre-school program.

Starting with the Transcendentalists and pioneers of infant school and nursery school movements, there is a continuity of historical events that follow social movements to our modern concept of a seamless continuity of schooling for all children from birth through the 12th grade.

6

Developing Literacy in Early Childhood

Urban societies, in all their breathtaking differences face a common task; transferring a range of skills, competencies, values, and sensibilities from one generation to the next. The socialization of the young is culturally defined, highly varied, and constantly evolving. If societies are to succeed, parents and guardians need to enable the next generation to carry on with the work of culture.

—Marcelo M. Suarez-Orozco (2005)

The emergence of language can have a profound effect on a learner's behavior. The acquisition of language brings into focus a power that the child has observed as possessed by others in family who were able to communicate their needs and wants at will. This magic was not accessible to the child until he or she accumulated a body of words and phrases to communicate his or her needs and wishes to others.

An observation of Piaget's stages will reveal that a highly useful vocabulary is usually available to children by their 30th month, and it grows rapidly. Start early. This is the response that should be given to caregivers, parents, and home schoolers, when they ask at what age they should start teaching literacy to children. Language learning starts with the first parent-child eye contact. If parents avoid eye contact with their infant, the infant will likely suspect that something is up, and that "something" is not good. It is essential that caregivers develop an unconditional positive relationship with infants in their care (Acredolo and Goodwyn, 1988).

During the first 12 months of life a persistent human quest is seeking attention from the caregiver. During the first months, babies are able to discriminate among speech sounds and can communicate nonverbally with caregivers. Before they are able to say their first words, children build on nonverbal communication they initiate earlier with their caregiver. It is essential that caregivers reach out to infants during their quest for the sharing of sounds (Adamson and Bakeman, 1984).

Around four years of age, children have usually acquired a highly useful working knowledge of the basic components of the language of their environment. Conversations with family members and others in the neighborhood have enabled their vocabulary to grow to approximately 4,000 words by 48 months of age.

Early interactive experiences with siblings, playmates, and caregivers create a transmission of in-group dialect. If this dialect is nonstandard, it is seldom rewarded when children enter school. This learning of a nonstandard dialect can be a downside of attachment behavior. Children interact with others in school, and they are expected to learn and use standard English during their schooling. Therefore, it is helpful when caregiver language and dialect are similar to the language and dialect spoken in school (McGee, 2003).

When the language of the caregiver and conversations in the home reinforce nonstandard dialect and this usage is necessary for social acceptance in both home and community, there can be conflict between standard dialect that is rewarded in school and the dialect of the neighborhood and family that is rewarded in the home (Bernstein, 1961).

This can be troublesome for some children because language is a conduit for humanistic values as well as academic ones. A dialect can be positively valued in the home, neighborhood, and friendship groups but negatively valued in school. And nonstandard English can be a barrier to academic acceptance (Labov, 2000).

If encouraged, children can practice the standard English dialect over a period of time and will often do so when it becomes clear to them that their social group negatively values their nonstandard dialect. It is also true, according to Labov (2000), that some nonstandard dialects are more persistent than others.

The caregiver has various roles in enabling the child to read and write. School systems have developed vocabulary lists and described reading competencies by grade level. There are various levels of grade-level reading and writing performance that are expected of school-age children. Parents, teachers, and home schoolers can be helpful in creating a child's comfort with reading, writing, and language usage prior to first grade (McGee, 2003).

These helpful periods can be divided into several encouraging encounters with children. This can include the sharing of books through reading and discussing, engaging in frequent conversations, encouraging and sharing ideas for artistic creative depictions, and assuming the role of *scribe* (a sibling or family adult writes what the nonreading child dictates), while encouraging children to write their own stories (Chall, 1987).

Children at this stage usually know the alphabet and letter sounds (the names of letters). They are ready to develop a sense of letter-sound skills and decode or "sound out" words not immediately recognized. This is called *phonemic awareness.* This is knowledge of how letters and words come together to make sounds and the sound of a printed letter or word. This is helped as children begin to recognize familiar words on street signs, commercial logos, and in newspapers, magazines, and books in the home. It is therefore important that a choice of periodicals and books be visible and accessible in the childcare center and home (Armbruster, 2003).

In language-rich environments, the child's decoding and phonic skills grow fast, and they should be encouraged to sound out words and try their skill at writing. Encourage them to label their artwork and describe to a listener (sibling or parent) what is happening. Their skills are growing at a fast pace, and their vocabulary will exceed their reading skill.

INTRODUCING STANDARD LANGUAGE AND DIALECT

Around 12 months of age, caregivers should encourage conversations using standard dialect. Such conversations should be frequent and long lasting. Caregivers occasionally lose patience with early language learners and respond with anger because of the child's repeated questions. For example, at a particular prereading stage, it might appear to an adult that children overuse the word *why* during conversations. Scolding or similar negative responses are inappropriate. During this prereading stage the caregiver should carry on conversations and read to children often. Children are learning the difference between real life that is represented in discussions and make-believe in stories and other print media.

Adults should pause in their reading when children ask questions or wish to discuss an aspect of the story. Here, conversations can be rich with discussions about values, morals, and problem solving, which at that time might be slightly above their intellectual level. Sometimes children will ask to have a particular story read to them many times. Occasionally, encourage children to "read" that particular book or story, encouraging them to turn the pages on their own. This will aid in building phonemic competence. Also assisting with phonemic competence are a number of books for children that use clever grammatical methods of repeating an initial sound in the same phrase or sentence. Representing this group is *Is Your Mama a Llama?* by Deborah Guarino (1997), also available in Spanish.

Phonemic awareness is also advanced when experiences from the child's real life are integrated with stories being read. Do not admonish the young reader for a misuse of or a misplacement of a word. As soon as feasible, the caregiver could use the word or phrase correctly in a comment or reply.

Parents should introduce children to the dramatic play of nursery rhymes as soon as they are able to sit alone, and encourage them to hold a small book as they are gradually taught to turn the pages. Start building a collection of books, including read-to nursery rhymes. Act out these rhymes in song and movement during patty-cake, lap, and sit-alone conversations. Young children's knowledge of nursery rhymes has been known to encourage early reading skills (Stuart et al., 1998; Doe, 1999; Rask, 2003). A useful summary of studies reviewing how nursery rhymes can encourage literacy learning and language development for multi-handicapped infants and toddlers can be found in studies reviewed by Glenn and Cunninghan (1984).

POST-PREREADING STAGE

When children have acquired some knowledge and insight into print and can recognize letters, common signs, and words like *it, the, and, to,* and *me,* often along with their name, and that print is read from left to right, learning to read is imminent. They will attempt to write their name and pretend that they can read a story that has been read to them often.

This pretending requires considerable basic knowledge. They know that the object they are holding is a book, and that is where stories are. They also know that reading is saying words in a pattern that is understandable to them and others, and that reading provides joy and captures their attention and moves across the page from left to right.

Many children in the post-prereading stage can write or recognize their name even when it has been written by others. They are able to speak and understand approximately 5,000 words. From observing the head movements of a caregiver reading to them, children at this stage often understand that words in the book are printed left to right, and occasionally the reader must turn the page. Paper, markers, crayons, and pencils should be visible and accessible for children to practice their writing and art.

A ROLE FOR A SCRIBE

At the third stage, the child will be able to understand a story and can discuss its major features in some manner, but might not be secure about her or his writing skills. The adult as *scribe* at the child's request will listen to a child's interpretation and write the most significant words spoken by the storyteller. This usually follows student-completed artwork that the caregiver integrates into the discussion of the story. The child will sign her or his name to the work.

At a later stage of development, children will be able to perform the art project of choice and request less assistance in writing. Later in a more advance stage the child will not need help with the writing or artistic representation, but might want to discuss the work.

CONVERSATIONS, DISCUSSIONS, AND A RESPECT FOR IDEAS

Before leaving this stage, have a discussion with early readers about the print that appears in the front of the book, like its title, name of the author, publication date, and the name of the publishing company.

Children should be invited to participate in discussions around them and practice words that are new to them. As children participate in language spoken around them, they will develop additional interest in reading, writing, and sharing their own stories. Occasionally, they will want artwork to accompany their tales. This is called *publishing*, and this word will be added to their vocabulary when used in discussing the child's *published* work. As children publish their work, the caregiver can be encouraging by asking important questions about the plot and related depictions.

For example, a child might write a single-sentence story like: *Tery got a bot (Terry Got a Boat)*. To display this idea, the child has a choice of drawing her or his version of a canoe, a sailboat, or fishing boat with oars. After the art project is completed, the caregiver *should not* remark, "What a beautiful boat" because here, the caregiver's remark suggests that adults are expert on the beauty of boats. Following such a comment, the child will then be in pursuit of graphic depictions that please the caregiver. After several experiences of this sort, the child's goal becomes one of pleasing the caregiver rather than a satisfaction with models of personal choice.

Let us consider a creative experience in terms of the relationship between the creator of art and the audience. The caregiver's discussion of the boat with its *creator* (the child) will transmit much about how it's valued by the child's *audience* (the caregiver).

A more encouraging response to the child from the caregiver or teacher would follow an adult question or similar remark, like "Tell me about this boat." The child's response could lead to a follow-up query that encourages more child/adult discussion. This interchange could continue as long as the adult is able to or wishes to capture the child's interest.

CHILDREN PUBLISHING

A child in the previous example has developed an idea for a book (story). With a little encouragement and support the child can expand on his or her ideas and offer the teacher an opportunity to discuss the publishing process and get the learner involved. Most schools have the materials and instructions. The instructions usually include the following steps:

1. The story can be written by the child or dictated to the teacher.
2. The editing phase is shared between the teacher and the writer of the story. Here, important learning experiences are derived from spelling and phrasing of ideas. Teachers must refrain from overextending influences on the main theme.
3. The finalized story is written by the author. Or, the author types the story. This can be done on a typewriter or computer. Here reading and spelling are practiced.
4. The bookbinding process is completed by the author. This can be done by covering the book with heavy-weight paper and stapling. Some schools have a binding kit with instructions for a more realistic book look.
5. The book title and author's name can be placed on the front along with designs (decoration?) of choice.
6. Information preceding the title page can have a dedication to a person of the author's choice (classmates, a friend, parents, or teacher).
7. Finally, the author should be recognized by placing the book in the class library or encouraging him or her to read the book to the class. Here, questions about the process of publishing, ideas for the story, and others can come from classmates.

EARLY LANGUAGE LEARNING

In the early 1900s when large numbers of Italian, Jewish, and Irish immigrant children entered public schools, calling attention to their dialect was a common ploy by experienced classmates to negatively value their presence. In part to avoid being singled out, schoolchildren from these families quickly adjusted to the standard language of the school. Their home neighborhood and grandparents however, retained some of the speech mannerisms that were common to their origins.

Children with foreign parents often spoke standard English in school and returned to a home where their family spoke Italian, Yiddish, or Irish dialect to parents and grandparents. French and German immigrants faced fewer language problems because these languages were positively valued and often included in the school curriculum. In fact, the first kindergarten in the United States was conducted in German (Swart, 1967).

Children in African American families that migrated from southern states to the north and Midwest also had difficulties with standard language adjustments in schools when their families moved to the "big city" to escape post-slavery conditions. White children migrating to states like California from failed farm communities in the 1920s and 1930s experienced similar problems.

Psycholinguists who study urban vernacular report that White ethnic groups adjust to standard dialectical variations and common grammatical styles with greater ease than African Americans. It is also reported that the linguistic transitions to standard English, regardless of their origin, are less likely to occur for a significant number of African American speakers (Labov, 2000).

For African Americans, discrimination in housing and employment meant fewer opportunities to practice standard English other than with speakers like themselves. It was not until 1965, for example, that discrimination in home ownership by the United States government was lifted. Prior to 1965, banks were informed by our government that mortgage loans granted to Blacks to purchase a home outside an area not already established as a Black neighborhood would not be guaranteed by the Federal Housing Administration. This pervasive practice trapped Black citizens in ghetto housing and urban housing projects, where classmates and often teachers were nonstandard English speakers like themselves.

What has been said about the entrance of new groups into American society does not apply to the largest set of population changes that have ever taken place in the large Northern cities of the United States: the arrival of great numbers of African Americans from the rural South, along with the rapid growth of the Hispanic population. So far, the sound changes sweeping across the United States have been portrayed as if they were general phenomena affecting to varying degrees all levels of the speech community. But this is not so. In Boston, New York, Philadelphia, Buffalo, Detroit, Cleveland, Chicago, San Francisco, and Los Angeles, the progress of the sound changes we have been studying stops short at the racial line. All speakers who are socially defined as white, mainstream, or Euro-American, are involved in the changes to one degree or another. There are leaders, and there rare followers, but in the mainstream community it is almost impossible to find someone who stands completely apart. But for those children who are integral members of a sub-community that American society defines as "non-white"—Black, Hispanic, or Native American—the result is quite different. No matter how frequently they are exposed to the local vernacular, the new patterns of regional sound change do not surface in their speech. On the deeper levels of syntax and semantics the African American community is carried even further away on a separate current of grammatical change, and a very sizeable fraction of the Hispanic speakers move with them. (Labov, 2000, p. 506)

ENVIRONMENTAL LITERACY

During common preschool experiences, children recognize that newspapers, magazines, and television are often integrated with what adults are "talking about." They also recognize that street signs, billboards, and other media print, like *Dunkin' Donuts, McDonald's, Burger King,* and the movie marquee, have meaning in our neighborhoods and are a part of "grown-up talk."

Talking to young children in phrases that encourage them to speak in return should be central to literacy initiatives. As babies babble and respond with their own choice of sounds, adults should respond with real words and phrases (Atkinson, MacWhinney, and Stoel, 1970). Here young children are learning that conversations mean many things; among them is taking turns.

Reading and math competencies of children in elementary, middle, and high school in most public systems demonstrate a need for improvement. However, when national mathematical skills of children in early-childhood grades in the United States are compared to the skills of their counterparts in other countries, U.S. children perform better than many. It is also true that this is not reported for literacy skills. These recent comparisons should not invite solace.

7

Play

A child who is healthy and physically comfortable will first employ himself in observing his surroundings, taking in the outer world, and playing, and working out his own life for himself. This dual activity of taking in the outer world and living out one's inner life is fundamental to his nature.

—Friedrich Froebel

It is likely that an examination of curriculum models taught in university teacher education programs and community-based early education programs will find play in the curriculum. This interest emerges from the influence of Friedrich Froebel's original kindergarten brought to the United States by his students. The concept of play, more often than not, has a meaning for the general public that is significantly different from Froebel's.

While well-educated teachers in early childhood have knowledge of the important implications of play in the lives of children, the general public's view is often one that interprets play as frivolity or something that children do to idle away their time.

This latter view has encouraged education planners, who are often not knowledgeable about its value, to remove play from essential curricula and replace it with paper-and-pencil seat work. Many in the general public have been willing to accept this curriculum replacement because the general public tends to view play as wasteful of valuable time when encouraged during the school day. Educators who have been early childhood practitioners and scholars express a different view.

Kindergarten used to mean brightly colored paintings, music, clay, block building, bursting curiosity, and intensive exploration. Now the kindergarten's

113

exuberance is being muted, its color drained . . . and spirit flattened, leaving us with stacks of paperwork and teacher manuals. No longer even designated "pre-school," kindergarten is becoming an adjunct to first grade, with workbooks replacing art materials and formal instruction replacing activities that follow the children's interest . . . They should be talking informally and in groups, looking at books and reading together, helping each other write signs and messages, playing out dramatic scenarios, telling stories and listening to others read and tell them. (Martin, 1985, p. 318)

This kindergartner's lament is for a kindergarten that builds upon the natural inclinations of children to participate actively in their own development. This active participation by children embodies a significant role for parents and teachers. Froebel encouraged parents and teachers to examine the memory of play from their own childhood. He emphasized that adults became aware of their environment through an understanding of the shape, texture, and meaning of objects and events in their surroundings. Through this meaning, adults acted upon their knowledge as a means of understanding themselves, their environment, and the outer world. For children, Froebel insisted, this meaning is achieved through their play. Children must work out their own lives through observations of natural events, and proceed to act out their *inner* demands (Froebel, 1900).

Froebel starts his concept of play as an essential part of the child's search for reality with the concept of a seed that has been planted. The earliest stage of development is occupied with the child's search for understanding of the *outer* world. The growing child's *inner* world seeks to know the environment, and this understanding is sought through the child's play. Froebel's kindergarten curriculum provides games and objects like a sphere (ball) and cube (square) to enhance the child's play. In the early stages of life, the child is unaware of his or her capacity and competency. It is, therefore, essential that adults provide objects, like a ball that can be grasped, bounced, kicked, held, or thrown, for example (Froebel, 1887).

By the 1960s, kindergarten curriculum materials included sets of wooden building blocks, music rhythm instruments, telephones, child-sized furniture with kitchen plates, servers, and utensils, dress-up clothing and art supplies for painting and drawing (Richter, 1937). These *play* objects represented what Froebel termed "gifts" in the 1800s. Froebel's gifts were durable objects. When placed in the use of children through curriculum implementation or the child's choice, *gifts* were deigned as objects of learning (Froebel, 1887).

As soon as a child is able to use his limbs and senses and to distinguish and identify sounds we should try to find for him a suitable object which he can grasp and hold. This child is aware of the unity which exists in all diversity and the object should express this. The child should see his own life reflected in its self-containment and its movement—though his awareness may not be at the conscious level—and be able to try out his ideas by means of such an object. This plaything is the sphere or ball. (Lange, 862–863, cited by Lilley, 1967, p. 99)

Froebel suggests that the child can understand how his or her own life is reflected in these self-motivated actions. They are termed self-motivated because the child's use of a "gift" is selected because of an *inner* drive to exercise certain skills and actions. In his capacity as a teacher of kindergartners, Froebel identifies the infant as a seed that eventually becomes a mature plant. With supportive care, the child's initial interaction is motivated toward the *outer* environment of objects and other people. This self-initiated inner activity is motivated to reach out. This reaching-out is an attempt to express "inner life" in an observable outward action. These outward responses, according to Froebel, display a latent understanding of self (Froebel, 1887). These outward responses are represented in Freud's oral stage, and can be provoked during infant assessments like *grasping, rooting, stepping,* and other reflexes that are described in the chapter on assessment.

Froebel's gifts and occupations were exciting concepts for the general public of the 1800s. Bolstered by this public interest, leaders in the kindergarten movement sought to increase kindergarten visibility. One selected venue was *The Philadelphia Exposition* of 1876. Here, they had built a model kindergarten classroom for display, and it attracted thousands of visitors to daily demonstrations and lectures.

In 2006, play as an essential feature remains in several early-childhood-education models. This valued position of play is found more in private education systems than in public ones. A great preponderance of public systems have blended elementary education with early childhood education and this has resulted in a group of modern classroom teachers without a sound valuing or knowledge of the role of play in child development.

It is also true that to prepare teachers for this blended model, large numbers of adjunct professors have been hired by universities on a part-time basis to train these new recruits. At the same time, some state education systems have implemented, while some others are planning, infant/toddler programs. It is expected that in these programs, *play* will be a significant part of the curriculum.

INFANTS AND TODDLERS

Infants are children from birth to 12 months. Toddlers are children from 12 months to 24 months of age. There are a variety of preschool child-care venues in most communities in the United States. Some are sponsored by and located in churches. Others are in private homes and for-profit centers, while others, like Head Start Centers and Early Head Start Centers, represent public policy and are sponsored by federally funded programs. There are also university-based child-care centers that provide experiences for students, and state-financed programs (some supported by lottery proceeds). There are also families that for various reasons decide to home-school their children.

As of this writing, local regulations for licensing in-home childcare are uneven and often inadequate to protect children from physical endangerment in unlicensed and licensed home care. Parents of children who have been victims of abuse by trained and untrained caretakers of infants, toddlers, and older children in their home are organizing to support legislation designed to prevent the physical endangerment of children. This parent-inspired activism is ongoing, and at this time too few states have instituted child-protection legislation for children in childcare.

THE DEVELOPMENT OF AGGRESSION

Caregivers who use physical punishment as a means of behavior modification and control are modeling these undesirable behaviors for all observing children who might interpret this approach as sanctioned by adults. Physical punishment is never recommended and by law must be reported when observed by an adult. Toddlers who observe adults interacting with others in this manner will assume that such behavior is approved, and children are likely to imitate such misbehaviors when they encounter conflicts.

It has been observed under various conditions that young children, predominantly males, prefer aggressive measures for resolving conflicts and tend to *behave like their country*. Students killing students have become too common in and around our schools. It should not surprise us that our youth identify with their country, especially during a time of war. Students in school today, along with their teachers, parents, and occasionally their grandparents, came into adulthood during the United States invasion of Vietnam (1965), the bombing of Cambodia (1970–1973), the invasion of Grenada (1983); and the invasion of Panama (1989). Children in schools today are growing up during the current U.S. invasion of Iraq.

There are various theories of behavior suggesting that learning is a *social process*. Theories that define learning as particularized through social forces have been proposed by Bronfenbruner (1979), Bandura (1986), and Vygotsky (1978). The works of these theorists are described in other areas of this text as *social learning theories*. Does the viewing of violent behavior influence violent behavior in the viewer? Is a positive correlation true for children and adults? Several studies directly and indirectly related to these question have been conducted (Vooijs and van der Vort, 1993; Valois and McKewon 1998).

J. Franzen, a New York City resident, writing about his deepest feelings that were called to consciousness by the first U.S. invasion of Iraq, offered the following:

> Deep in my Queens neighborhood . . . ugly news had reached me through the twin portals of my TV set and my *New York Times* subscription. The country was preparing for war ecstatically, whipped up by William Safire (for whom Saddam Hussein was "this generation's Hitler") and George Bush ("vital issues of principle are at stake"), whose approval rating stood at 89 percent. In the righteousness of the country's hatred of a man who until recently had been our close petropolitical ally, as in the near total absence of political skepticism about the war, the United States seemed to be as terminally out of touch with reality as Austria had been in 1916, when it managed to celebrate the romantic "heroism" of mechanized slaughter in the trenches. I saw a country dreaming of infinite oil for its hour-long commutes of glory in the massacre of faceless Iraquis, of eternal exemption from the rules of history. . . . I began to think that the most reasonable thing for a citizen to do might be to enter a monastery and pray for humanity. (Franzen, 1996, p. 35)

Following the U.S. invasion of Panama in 1989 when the U.S. military killed an estimated 3,000 Panamanian civilians, there was an increase in children bringing guns to school. Increases of such incidents are not altogether unusual following their country's invasion of another country.

During the U.S. invasion of Panama, it was reported that our military was after one man, Manuel Noriega. Our bombers destroyed one of the most impoverished Panamanian communities, killing more than 3,000 of its citizens, and bulldozed the civilian casualties that our forces killed into mass graves. Panamanian citizens were unable to locate their missing kin because initially the existence and location of the graves were kept secret (Ryan, 1993; Gilboa, 1995). How our country resolves its problems through military invasions of smaller countries has implications for how our children relearn to solve theirs. And as of 2005 our country has not signed the UN Convention on the Rights of the Child (Neuman, 2005).

The Panama story is made more complex in part because Noriega was at one time employed by the U.S. government to spy on Central and South American countries (Dinges, 1991). After the invasion, the U.S. authorities wanted to portray Noriega as a villain to justify their invasion and massacre of Panamanians. To support this scenario, the U.S. Southern Command told reporters, who subsequently printed the story, that 110 pounds of cocaine were found in Noriega's Panamanian residence. A month later the incriminating "cocaine" was found to be *tamales,* a favorite Panamanian food (Cook and Cohen, 1990).

Currently, our president is being downgraded in public polls because a significant percentage of U.S. citizens opposed his congressionally authorized invasion of Iraq. According to some, the invasion was to ensure the U.S. supply of oil, while the president has stated that the purpose was to destroy Iraq's supply of "weapons of mass destruction." By now, the claim that Iraq possessed such weapons at the time of the invasion has been proven inaccurate.

Accurate counts of Iraqi citizens killed during the U.S. invasion are difficult to obtain, but most independent reporting agencies agree that civilian deaths are in excess of 30,000 children and adults. During the U.S. occupation of Iraq, an annual rate of over 100 children a year have brought guns to school in the United States.

Recently, two students in the Quincy, Massachusetts, schools were charged with writing bomb threats, bringing a gun to school, and planting grenades (Sears, 2005). In Texas, a five-year-old took a loaded gun to school that was eventually taken from him by a fifth grader (Hill, 2005). According to an eight-year-old boy, he brought a gun to school because he was being bullied (Associated Press Wire, 2004).

A 13-year-old student was charged with a felony in Spokane, Washington, after a gun that he was suspected of bringing to school was found stashed in the boys' restroom (McDonald, 2005). It should not surprise us that children who bring guns to school are mostly males, both Black and White, but rarely females or Asian Americans. Children bringing guns to school are representative of the military mix that children observe on their family's TV news hour. To what extent do war behaviors enacted by their country become assumed behaviors by maturing young men (Bandura's, Bronfenbrenner's, and Vygotsky's *social learning theories*)?

On May 20, 1998, after 15 year old Kipland Philip Kinkel was expelled for bringing a gun to school, he shot and killed his father, and later his mother. On May 21, 1998, he drove his mother's car to Thurston High School in Springfield, Oregon. He carried a semi-automatic rifle, a .22 caliber automatic pistol, his father's 9mm Glock pistol, and a hunting knife strapped to his leg. As he entered his high school's hallway, he shot student Ben Walker in the head. He then shot another student, Ryan Atteberry.

He then entered the cafeteria and opened fire, injuring other children. He shot Mikael Nicholauson, who had already received a bullet in his thigh and another in his chest, in the head at point blank range. After receiving a shot to the abdomen, 17-year old Jake Ryker heard a sound that was familiar to him from his youth marksmanship instruction training given by the National Rifle Association. It was the click of a gun when it is temporarily out of ammunition. Seizing this opportunity, Jake, along with other students, Adam Walburger, and Doug and David Ure, subdued Kip Kinkel and held him until authorities took control.

Nicholauson died at the scene. Walker, after being transported to the hospital, died after being kept on life support until both parents arrived. Other students, including Jake Ryker were taken to the hospital with a variety of wounds.

Kip Kinkel was on Ritalin, a psychotropic medication often prescribed for behavior modification. The only psychiatrist who had seen Kinkel before the shootings maintained that he was in satisfactory mental health. When brought to the police station, Al Warthen, a police officer, said that Kinkel lunged at him with a knife for what he surmised was an attempt to provoke him to shoot Kinkel. Instead, Warthen immobilized Kinkel with pepper spray.

Kinkel now serves a life sentence at the MacLaren Youth Correctional Facility, a facility for boys located in Woodburn, Oregon. (*Wikipedia*, 2006)

In addition to *social learning theories* that are pertinent to this discussion, Freud has suggested that there are fundamental human characteristics served by group attractions represented through membership in what he calls "artificial groups."

In a Church (and we may with advantage take the Catholic Church as a type) as well as an army, however different the two may be in other respects, the same illusion holds good there being a head—in the Catholic Church Christ, in an army its Commander-in-Chief who loves all the individuals in the group with an equal love. Everything depends upon this illusion; if it were to be dropped, then both Church and army would dissolve, so far as the external force permitted them to. . . . He stands to the individual members of the group of believers in the relation of a kind elder brother; he is their substitute father. (Freud, 1965, p. 33)

David Luban, in an article titled "Torture, American-Style" (2005), asks his readers to contemplate the following:

Consider the cases of Abed Hamed Mowhoush and Manadel Jamadi. Mowhoush, an Iraqi general in Saddam Hussein's army was smothered to death in a sleeping bag by U.S. interrogators in western Iraq. Jamadi, a suspected bomb-maker, whose repacked body was photographed at Abu Ghraib, was seized and roughed-up by Navy SEALS in Iraq, then turned over to the CIA for questioning. At some point during this process . . . someone broke his ribs; then he was hooded and underwent "Palestinian hanging" until he died. . . . Shamefully, (the American) system that permits cruel, inhuman and degrading treatment, smudges long-standing lines about what is and is not, permitted in routine interrogations—and then expresses hypocritical horror when soldiers and interrogators cross the blurry line into torture and murder. (pp. 22–23)

Despite the behavior of our country and our preoccupation with war and guns, our children *must be taught* to resolve conflicts in a nonviolent manner. And, in addition to family adults, teachers and caregivers are in a strategic position to assure that this is done. When children encounter aggression, they must resolve all conflicts in an atmosphere of nonaggression. Children should be informed that when confrontations are beyond their control, an adult they trust should be summoned to the scene. It is the caregiver's role to teach and demonstrate nonviolent procedures for conflict resolution (Valois and McKewon, 1998).

A common incident arises in preschool when a child is playing with a one-of-a-kind toy for what, in another child's view, is an unreasonable long period of time. When a different child offers a reasonable request to borrow that toy and is rejected by the child now in possession of the toy, the teacher should encourage the children to resolve the dispute themselves. The teacher can suggest that they work it out through time sharing, for example, just to get a negotiating discussion started. The teacher should remain in sight and hearing distance of the negotiating process. If it does not go well, the teacher should reenter the conflict-resolution process and assume an insider's role.

Sometimes a major part of a day in child-care centers is spent in resolving conflicts. And often, if given a modest amount of help, children are able to negotiate their own disagreements on satisfactory terms of nonviolent agreements. Most of all, oral negotiating can avoid pushing, tugging, and hitting strategies that children sometimes employ in conflict resolution. Disagreements will occur, and they often provide opportunities for children to develop nonaggressive, positive, problem-solving skills, while the teacher remains on the scene as an informing observer.

Occasionally, there will be a child who reaches such an extreme state of frustration that he or she will attempt to or will actually bite or hit another child. There are various ways to assure the safety of other children from "biters." Some programs refuse enrollment to children who bite and/or repeat such acts. If your workplace has a policy of allowing such children to attend the program, plans toward modifying such behavior must start with a conversation with the parents of the offending child.

Chances are, the parent is already aware of the child's aggressive behaviors. Inquire as to the parent's knowledge of such behavior, and if any professional recommendations are on record. From this knowledge, the teacher must work out a plan with the parent to assure the safety of the offender and other children. If the offending child is in treatment, recommendations should be requested from the therapist by parents and shared with the teacher. Do not ignore any acting out of this type that has the potential of harming other children.

When biting is only an occasional act, it can be helpful to suggest that the parent buy a rubber pacifier ring and place it on a string around the offending child's neck. Tell the child; "When you become frustrated or angry and want to bite something, bite your neck ring."

Herrenkohl and Russo (2001) have reported that manifestations of aggression in early childhood are likely to signal the beginning of similar problems later in adulthood. They also suggest that minor aggression can indicate inclinations toward more serious violence later in life. Information concerning negative behaviors of their children could be suggested reading for parents.

There are various ways in which children can practice problem solving by solving problems with the teacher's help during a normal daytime activity. One example of problem solving occurs when adults assist children in putting things away during cleanup time. This is not always an attractive activity for children or adults. When adults participate in helping the group remove building blocks from the floor or assist in reorganizing small parts in boxes, or placing things on shelves following a busy morning, this is getting the aggravating "problem" of cleaning up out of the way. The problem-solving process has been built into various early-childhood curriculum approaches. One prominent integration of problem-solving methods with regular early-childhood learning activities was introduced in the early 1900s, called *The Project Method.*

THE PROJECT METHOD

Introduced in the early 1900s, an interactive method of teaching and learning in early childhood practice was called *The Project Method.* There are several variations that can be enacted from a common objective. The central approach is designed to include several domains of knowledge: mathematics, reading, writing, social studies, science, and other areas of knowledge that might emerge from the creativity and interaction of children engaged in a single project.

For example, let us suppose that a second-grade class, following a story discussed by the teacher and the class, creates a strong interest among the learners about their town. During the discussion several children suggest a project that they build a model of downtown. As their plans advance, it is suggested that they could construct models of the downtown park, their movie theater, the church, and the food market. One child suggests that his family has a large cardboard box in which their new refrigerator came. Other children chime in and volunteer to bring in other paraphernalia that might be of use.

The teacher suggests that each child make a sketch (art) of the section and buildings of downtown that should be represented in their project (social studies), and write a single-page essay as to why they made their selections (reading, writing). This can be followed by a presentation of ideas to the entire group by each child (publishing).

By this time, the class has met in small groups and has had time to make choices and decide on sections of the plan. Finally, the small committees are brought together with the teacher to decide on a master plan (cooperative learning). Things like cardboard, sections of wood, and related start-up materials can be brought in from home by children or secured from local merchants, like a lumber yard, for example.

As construction proceeds, a child might suggest that their food market, movie house, and jewelry store need signs to inform customers about their products (writing). Another child might suggest that it will be dark inside the buildings, so they will need lights inside the stores. Flashlight batteries and bulbs can be obtained from any hardware store along with the necessary sockets and wiring (science).

In 1915, when the project method was labeled *project teaching*, its first description was published by J. A. Randall. The following year, David Snedden expanded the project concept in *School and Society* (1916). Gradually, the project method started to attract educators in specific study areas beyond early childhood education (von Hofe, 1916; Woodhull, 1919). Revived in the late 1980s by Katz and Chard, today the project method can be found in various early-childhood settings around the world.

Our advocacy of the project approach is rooted in our own ideological commitments and values related to the aims of education. An overall aim of this approach is to cultivate the life of the young child's mind. In its fullest sense, the term mind includes not only knowledge and skills, but also emotional, moral and aesthetic sensibilities. . . . Let us begin with a quick look at project work in progress in an early childhood classroom: Several children are collaborating on a painting, depicting what they have learned about the driving mechanism of the school bus. Their teaching is helping them label the steering wheel, horn, gearshift, ignition, accelerator, hand brake, brake pedal, turn indicators, windshield wipers, and inside and outside rearview mirrors.

A small group is working on felt pen drawings of parts of the motor, indicating where oil and water are added. The children make a diagram showing how fuel flows from the gas tank to the motor and how the exhaust makes its way through the tailpipe. As they work, they correct each other and make suggestions about what goes where and what details to include.

A third small group is finishing a display of their paintings showing the different kinds of lights inside and outside of the bus. The display notes which lights are for signals and warnings and which serve to light the way ahead as well as inside. Some lights are red, some are amber, and some white, some flash on and off, and some are just reflectors. Their work is accompanied by a lively exchange of information and opinion about what they have seen and how to picture it so that other children can see what they mean.

A fourth group has prepared a chart of gauges and dials on the dashboard, giving a basic idea of the information each one yields. Two of the children used a rope to establish the width and length of the bus. They have displayed their rope on a counter in front of a sign the teacher helped them write (Katz and Chard, 1989, pp. 1–2).

The developing interest in the *project method,* originally introduced by early-childhood educators, gradually attracted the attention of teachers in elementary and secondary education. Grade-school teachers in general were in the midst of organized changes. This gave rise to what became known as *Progressive Education.*

Progressive education was a movement guided by the theories of John Dewey and William Kilpatrick. This new trend in education, inspired primarily by Dewey's child-centered approach to education, was a reaction to structured teacher-centered approaches.

Anyone attending grade school in the United States prior to the 1950s can describe a system of rigid authoritarian control that required quiet student attention. This was the typical classroom environment that the progressive-education movement intended to change.

For those students fortunate enough to attend high school, their curriculum was designed as preparation for university studies. The new system of progressive education encouraged teachers to appreciate students as active, insightful thinkers and to encourage them to participate in their own learning.

Progressive educators suggested that rigid approaches to conducting classroom learning actually stalled the acquisition of knowledge because teacher-centered approaches ignored the creativity of students anxious to test what they have learned in an open, active forum with peers and teachers.

By 1915, William Kilpatrick supported a more interactive role for learners along the lines of the then-current arguments favoring progressive-education curriculum. Gradually, planners were involved in an expansion of curriculum approaches that included students in discussing, planning, and judging the content of their classroom activities. Several educators expanded this new vision for the classroom and extended the curriculum to include community projects.

In an effort to integrate various child-centered curriculum approaches of that time and promote a broad-based theory of progressivism in education, Kilpatrick planned to use the *project method* as a centerpiece of his academic endeavors (1918). Dewey's philosophy, though in line with these emerging child-centered interests in student and teacher freedoms to learn, surprised some converts by insisting that a clearly articulated purpose must be a part of any classroom/learning academic lesson or project. It was common practice to ignore Dewey's recommendations for rigor because his writings were complex and an especially formidable task for classroom teachers of the 1920s to comprehend. The academic training attained by many classroom teachers of that time was generally modest.

Despite several problems with instituting a more liberal approach to curriculum that resembled what had already been achieved in kindergarten, the introduction of Kilpatrick and Dewey methodologies did influence more open classroom approaches. From the central core of *Progressive Education* and the *Project Method,* a number of common themes were spun off from Progressive Education, like *The Open Classroom, The Learning Community, Humanistic Education, Cooperative Learning, Project Teaching, The Discovery Method,* and *Schools Without Walls,* which could be found in school settings and educational literature years later (Maslow, 1968; Rogers, 1969; Jones, 1970; Morgan, 1973).

PARENTAL SELECTION OF CHILDCARE

Families deciding not to care for infants and toddlers at home should, before enrolling them in a child-care center, visit the center(s) of choice at different times during the day to observe their services. Areas of interest should include finding out about transportation, safety, child-teacher ratio, the quality and quantity of indoor and outdoor equipment, materials, furniture, fixtures, and the building structure. A full-day visit to observe activities related to how children are learning and how they are treated over a full day will also be helpful.

The training and credentials of the staff, though important, can vary considerably. The basic requirement is often high school completion. For centers with workers who have training beyond high school, it is important to know the *type* of training they have had.

There are important differences between program quality of care found in preschool programs with a well-trained staff on the one hand, and staff with minimum training on the other. Parents should also inquire about the educational level of the supervisory staff.

The program director should have a four-year college or university degree in early-childhood education. At a minimum, teachers should have two years of child study. More often than not, these two years will have culminated in an AA (associate's of arts) degree. Occasionally, the two years will be the length of time a worker has spent in an incomplete pursuit of a four-year Bachelor's degree, and the two years of study in this instance is not equal to an AA degree.

When a teacher completes an AA degree in child care, the two-year period is a terminal degree study involving the practical instruction and care of young children. An applicant who has completed two years of a four-year degree in early-childhood education, for example, has completed two years of general education *for the teacher,* with little or no study related to early-childhood practice. It is in the remaining two years of this latter applicant's four-year program that a concentration in the *study of the practice* of early-childhood education will occur.

Therefore, when examining the academic credentials of a child-care program's teaching staff, it is important to know that even though a four-year degree is more desirable than a two-year degree, a person who has completed the first two years of a four-year program is not as suitable as a teacher who has completed a two-year AA degree in child care, when both teachers have two years of training. It can also be helpful to know if the teaching staff is continuing their training through workshops and conferences. This is desirable, and notices of these experiences are often posted in the child-care center.

Head Start programs since 1995 have required a minimum of an AA degree for their teachers; however, few programs had reached this goal as of 2006. As of this writing, Early Head Start caregivers who work full time with infants are often local mothers with a high school diploma. Many workers with minimum credentials, however, perform commendably. They can provide attentive and competent child care, and a one-day visit and observation should relieve any parent's concerns (Rust, 1993).

Being cared for at home is usually the most desirable environment for infants, especially for the first six weeks of life. It is recommended that infants not start full-day center-based programs until after six weeks of age.

By three months of age the average infant will more than likely be able to lift up her head when lying on her stomach. At the end of 4 1/2 months, she will be able to roll over, and sit without support by eight months. By the age of 11 months the average infant will be able to stand alone while holding on to furniture, and walk by holding on at 14 months. A few weeks after standing alone, the toddler will be walking, and by 22 months she will be able to walk up stairs while holding on.

There can be a month-long difference between the performance of infants and toddlers who achieve age-appropriate motor skills. Because environments vary, some infants and toddlers have greater opportunities for interaction and greater motivation for achieving milestones, with the presence of more same-age children who have successfully reached an advanced mark.

Infants and toddlers in some center-based programs might reach gross motor milestones earlier than children raised in a single-child household or confined to a playpen for long periods during waking hours, for example. Reaching these milestones within a range of two to three weeks is natural, and caregivers should not be alarmed if an infant or toddler's performance does not meet the averages noted previously (Schickedanz, 1997).

Each infant should have his or her name on a large 8" by 12" envelope (or suitable file) containing up-to-date medical notes on health, feeding instructions from home, and related matter, along with any special instructions from the parent. Workers should become familiar with this information at the beginning of each day and prior to taking an infant out of doors.

INFANTS

In the child-care center the infant room should contain four separate areas, each area appropriate for the number of infants to be housed there: (1) A sleeping area with cribs, one labeled for each child. (2) A changing area. All workers must wash hands after each change procedure, prior to leaving the change area. Have a supply of disposable rubber gloves at hand. (3) An eating area with a place for infants to be held, with enough room for older infants to sit or crawl about. (4) A play area with colorful age-appropriate materials designed to meet the needs of active infants at the earlier and older stages of development. It is considered appropriate for some areas to be large enough to satisfy a dual use when the staff understands and accepts this arrangement. For example, areas three and four can satisfy dual use.

Infants should be taken outdoors periodically as weather allows. Center staff should read medical notes and parent's instructions prior to transitions (like outdoor activities following a diaper change or feeding). After certainty that medical notes and parent information are confirmed, infants should be taken outside to areas landscaped for this purpose. The area should include variations of shade and sun, low-cut grass, and clean concrete free of small stones, pebbles, and bits of glass. A safe ground cover that includes flowers and/or a garden should be visible and accessible.

Infant outdoor areas can also include appropriate-size swings, low climbing structures covered with soft material, and a play area with appropriate commercial and homemade toys. Infant activities must be conducted under strict safety supervision in accordance with infant safety and care. A child-care worker must be present for every three children at all times. Workers should be alert to safety factors. Repair needs like damaged swings, for example, should be reported and repaired prior to next use (Hohmann and Weikart, 1995).

INDOOR ENVIRONMENTS FOR TODDLERS

Environment: A day room should be large enough for the group of children who are being supervised there. Furniture, fixtures, games, and toys should be arranged in a manner that gives full visibility for caretakers to all parts of the room. The day rooms should contain an accessible bathroom where adults can take children, and some older toddlers will be encouraged to get used to the idea. There should be tables for feeding/eating and play areas for toddlers who are near 24 months. An area of the room should be divided into art, blocks, books, manipulable objects, science table, sand table, water table, dramatic and play area, and an area for interactive and large-motor activities, along with a writing area with nearby flat surfaces, nontoxic crayons and markers, along with paper (Salot, 1965).

The Art Area

This area should contain paper, nontoxic paste and markers, play dough, non-pointed safe plastic scissors, paper of different textures and colors, small patches of cloth, and flat crayons.

The Book Area

Sturdy hardcover picture books that can be cleaned with a damp cloth, books placed strategically around a toddler-height table with comfortable chairs, nearby area(s) where toddlers can retreat for semiprivacy adjoining a soft floor carpet that allows the caretaker to read a "group story" when appropriate. Diversity in family and neighborhoods should be displayed and openly available for children and staff (Hixon, 1982).

Construction Area

Self-start, age-appropriate games, three- or four-piece puzzles that do not require adult supervision. Nesting toys, wood hammer and pounding boards, a set of hollow blocks, tabletop and floor light plastic building blocks, stacking toys, and large beads for stringing should be visible and accessible.

Dramatic Play Area

Dress-up clothing on hangers, mirror(s), several telephones, a child-safe record player with a few records, dolls of various ethnicities and gender, a cradle, a few stuffed animals and small musical instruments (tambourine, maracas, etc.), all inviting role play, including low shelf furniture for storing flat objects during cleanup time.

Sand and Water Tables

Either one or both should be available, including measuring containers and scoops. This activity requires alert supervision, not direct control. The water/sand table should be placed in a nontraffic area because of the likelihood that sand and water will spill on the floor.

Floor Covering in Activity Rooms

Program planners do not always agree about appropriate floor covering in activity rooms. Ages of the children who make use of an activity area are an important factor to take into account. Carpeted floor areas with a generous space for large sitting-on toys, wagons, push toys, step-up blocks, and building blocks are preferred by some planners, while others suggest floors covered with hard (wood or linoleum) material that can be completely cleaned daily. A preferred alternative would be a tight, flat-woven, solid-colored carpet with a good resistance to spilled liquids. Carpet of this style is commercially available in patterns with child-care motifs especially designed for preschool settings. This latter floor covering requires daily cleaning maintenance.

TODDLERS' OUTDOOR ACTIVITY

Materials and equipment should be developmentally appropriate. Check for medical notes and parent instructions for each child prior to going outside. The outdoor area should be accessible and include variations of shade and sun, low-cut grass, and clean concrete free of small stones, pebbles, and bits of glass. A safe ground cover including flowers and/or a garden should be visible and accessible.

Activities in the outdoor area can include age-size swings, low climbing structures, a playhouse, see-saw and slide, tricycles and other age-appropriate riding toys, and a sand box where toys can be included. Attention and care should be provided by the same individual on a daily basis as this is important for maintaining a continuity of caregiver-child relationships and future development (Hohmann and Weikart 1995).

At a minimum, one child-care worker for every three toddlers should be in the child's presence at all times. Workers should also be alert to safety factors. Daily inspections of outdoor equipment could reveal repair needs like damaged swings, for example, and should be reported for repair prior to next use.

As children practice their walking skills they often hold on to furniture and other upright objects. Caretakers should be alert to sharp objects and unstable uprights along the toddler's pathway. Caring for infants and toddlers is also integrated with the caregiver's teaching. As adults move around in the work area, caregiving should be accompanied by discussions with infants and toddlers about objects in the physical environment and their actions that are taking place. It is during this time that children can be taught safety procedures and directed away from dangerous pitfalls.

Caregivers should use the aforementioned ideas as a general guide to learning environments for infants and toddlers. They should also use their own creativity and a thoughtful sense of safety in placing furniture, fixtures, materials, and playthings that reflect the needs, interests, and ages of children in the program. By the age of two, for example, children need large open spaces that are free of fixtures not useful or intended for their benefit.

Beyond the age of two, children's awareness moves beyond egocentrism to a concern for others. Erikson identifies this stage with the childhood period of moving beyond self-doubt to a sense of autonomy (Erikson, 1950). Piaget defines this as a period of child development that passes through egocentrism (Piaget, 1952). From Friedrich Froebel we know that childhood experiences in open spaces with playthings and objects of interest (Froebel called them "gifts") contribute to the child's awareness and knowledge of the outside world (1900).

Children's play also informs parents and teachers about the types of opportunities more likely to make children aware of their bodies in climbing, skipping, hopping, and running. Often such muscle-developing activity during free play will be started by one child who will soon be joined by others, and it gradually builds into a *group activity.*

This march can attract other playmates with thoughtful ideas of their own. A contagious interest could gradually include a tambourine, maracas, drum, or a child-constructed music maker or rhythm instrument. This activity, originating with the engagement of a single child, can advance rather quickly into a "marching band," and combine body movement, interaction, creative thinking, spontaneity, planning, and the creation of rhythms (Vernazza, 1981).

8

The Future of Early-Childhood Education

It is the lucid vertigo of a language that is trying to redefine the world while it redefines itself in the full knowledge that, in an age that is still uncertain, the key to the revelation of the world can be found not in the straight line but only in the labyrinth.

—Umberto Eco

One of the most critical experiences in our lives is the transition from the supportive comforts of family life to a classroom full of competitive children our age. This transit brings into focus a set of human imperatives that never before required our attention. It is also true that this dramatic change makes it essential that expectations for learner performance that have been formulated by child-development theorists are coordinated with what is known about child growth and development from birth through age eight.

Starting with the first day of school, curriculum requirements established by thoughtful planning in the various learned societies must be implemented in the manner of continuity and care.

To improve on an uneven statewide inclusion of kindergartens in public schools in the early 1900s, a consistent vigil was necessary to align curriculum across ages to assure a continuity of children's knowledge acquisition. Likewise, similar attention is required as emerging federal and local public policy initiatives are creating infant/toddler programs.

There are persistent signs that state and federal educational initiatives are moving in the direction of creating a public educational system that will eventually provide public schooling for children from birth (six weeks) through grade 12. It is difficult to predict when this transition will be completed, but Early Head Start, a federally supported early-education program for infants six weeks to age two is a major experimental project and is available to families of low and moderate income. Public school planners are supporting initiatives that provide preschool education and care starting in infancy (Table 3.2).

In their view, this policy will assist in creating a more knowledgeable school-ready group of kindergarten children.

In addition to federally funded experimental programs, there presently exist proprietary preschool programs that are offered on a fee basis. In light of these developments, the labyrinth of public policy agencies, sometimes not knowing what each is doing, has ignored public policy initiatives that might reduce the involvement of extended families in the child-care picture. In this regard, child-supportive services now provided for young children by their grandparents, aunts, and uncles, and other extended family members may be less available after 2006. Recently, federal tax policies have been modified to eliminate tax deductions for extended-family members acting as caregivers.

As organized schooling inches toward expanding early education for infants and toddlers, teachers and administrators will require certification for serving this age group. It is expected that additional requirements will be put in place for the schooling of infants and toddlers.

Accrediting agencies that are generally accepted by university-based teacher-education programs and state education agencies that certify classroom teachers do so in a K–12 model (see Table 3.1). Learned societies that establish an approach to work for planners and practitioners responsible for this model include the *National Council for the Accreditation of Teacher Education*, the *National Board for Professional Teaching Standards*, and the *Interstate New Teacher Assessment and Support Consortium*. These agencies accredit university-based teacher-education programs; visit, evaluate, and certify education institutions of higher learning; and make recommendations to university-based course offerings that are required of teacher candidates.

Aside from teacher licensure recommendations and periodical on-site examinations of teacher-education programs, there are occasional meetings between the aforementioned agencies to coordinate their work toward the betterment of teaching, teacher education, the education of children, and professionalism in the field of education. Their most recent report for young learners was issued in 2005 under the title *Program Standards for Elementary Teacher Preparation Part 1: Standards for Candidates Preparing to Teach Elementary Education Students.*

Their report ignored children younger than three (infants and toddlers). It is also noteworthy that the report concerned "elementary education" and not "early-childhood education." This trend is designed to gradually blend the discipline of *early-childhood education* into *elementary education* and gradually eliminate the use of traditional early-childhood initiatives.

Historically, early-childhood education and the care of infants and toddlers have been identified by the *age* of children (birth through age eight), and elementary education has traditionally been identified by the child's *grade* (K–6). Early-childhood education and development remains unlike K–12 schooling in that it is uniquely diverse. In a national context, early-childhood education and related services are provided in a variety of settings, some for profit, some operated in public schools, church settings, and on university campuses primarily for preservice teacher training, and child and family services like Early Head Start and Head Start centers (Table 3.1). Michelle J. Neuman places early-childhood education, care, and public policy, in a global context:

> There are two main national approaches to governance: *divided* and *integrated*. In most countries, public responsibility for early care is administratively divided between "care" for children under age three and "education" for preschoolers. In Belgium, France, Italy, and the Netherlands, for example, free universal preschool for children from age three or four is part of the public education system, under the ministry of education, whereas fee-based early care services for infants and toddlers (often with working or at-risk parents) are the responsibility of health and social affairs ministries. Within divided systems, there may be several ministries with parallel and over-lapping responsibilities for same age groups of children (e.g., Japan, Australia, and the U.S.). In the U.S., for example, 69 federal programs, under nine federal agencies and departments, provided or supported education and care for children under five in 1999. (Neuman, 2005, p. 189)

When *elementary education* was first theorized for public education, *kindergartens* were being conducted in philanthropic and community-based social institutions. Some cities invited kindergartners, their curriculum, and their students, to move into their school buildings as a separate offering for families. Kindergarten advocates that accepted these invitations were charged rent. As described elsewhere in this text, it was not until the late 1890s that a few cities started to provide tax-supported public kindergarten education (that later became a part of early-childhood education), to precede the first three grades (called primary grades). This left the vast number of public schools in the United States still without free kindergartens in public schools.

In some cities without kindergartens, affluent parents petitioned for local public school kindergartens. After successfully achieving education for children younger than six, such state-mandated services were eventually made a permanent part of elementary education programs in most U.S. communities

Several public policy initiatives for public schooling, however, did not mandate kindergartens for many areas across the nation. In Georgia, for example, the state education department, over the objections of many taxpaying parents, did not *mandate* public kindergartens until the 1980s. By 2005, kindergarten attendance was still not *required* in Georgia. However, six-year-olds entering school for the first time must achieve a passing grade on an entrance examination to avoid *mandatory* kindergarten attendance, regardless of their age.

Today, many state-issued reports confuse the grade/age categories by failing to distinguish *early-childhood education* from *elementary education* (Table 3.1). Too often, practitioners and planners (many of whom are political appointees) do not know the difference. There are two national learned societies responsible for disseminating policy matters concerning early childhood practices; they are *The National Association for the Education of Young Children* and *The Association for Early Childhood Education International*, and they have consistently reported that early-childhood education spans the ages of *birth to through eight* (Table 3.1).

Early-childhood learned societies bring our attention to the need for teacher educators and program planners to be sensitive to the transitional periods of early childhood, when learners are moving from home to preschool, and later from third to fourth grade in regular school (Fabian and Dunlop, 2002).

Along the pathway to a *realistic* identification of the early-childhood field of study, there are various obstacles, some *political,* some *theoretical,* and some *economic.* Political obstacles include persons who achieved *elementary-education* training and are securely entrenched in policy-making state education departments. For the most part, this group has been educated in *elementary education* but contracted and bestowed with the title of *early-childhood educators.*

At best, some of the administrators who hired them were trapped in similar circumstances; at worst, hiring administrators were not aware that there was a difference between *early childhood* and *elementary education.* Joining this group are those with *middle-grades* training, a designation that has been drifting out of vogue for some time now. Some of these educators have moved into the lower grades (6–9), of secondary education.

Also confusing the state-designated categories of early childhood/elementary education are local school superintendents who prefer to recruit teacher-education graduates with *early-childhood* certification over graduates with *elementary/middle grades* certification to teach K–8 children in their schools.

Economic concerns tend to surface when university administrators seek a place for tenured elementary/middle-school/secondary professors whose courses have become less in demand. A common practice is to assign these professors to teach courses and supervise student teachers in reading education, special education, and early-childhood education.

In too many education departments *early-childhood* vacancies are filled with *elementary education/middle-grades*-trained professors. These professors will, more often than not, select people with backgrounds similar to their own, when they are hired and become members of faculty recruitment committees. This gradual process will eventually make a mockery of university departments of *early-childhood education.* Improvements will come when the problem is *recognized* by university academics and administrators. They must have the *courage* and the *resources* to recruit candidates who have been educated in the *history, philosophy, theory,* and *practice of early-childhood education.*

Glossary

accommodation: According to Jean Piaget, the process through which existing ideas and skills are modified to fit new experiences and ideas.

adaptation: According to Jean Piaget, a designation for the process of development where concepts are expanded and deepened through assimilation and modified by accommodation.

amniocentesis: A procedure that examines whether a fetus has certain genetic disorders.

anal stage: According to Sigmund Freud, that stage in sexual development (9–16 months) in which the center of pleasure shifts to the anus and to activities related to elimination.

animism: According to Piaget, the tendency for young children to assume that inanimate objects such as clouds have the properties of living things, like feelings and thoughts.

Apgar score: A neonatal health rating immediately following birth that is based on heart rate, breathing, strength, muscle tone, color, and reflex responsiveness.

approach behaviors: Neonatal behaviors that establish and maintain physical *closeness with caregivers.* This closeness includes sucking on the fist, smiling, and clinging.

aptitude test: Measurement of the capacity for future performance in a selected area of behavior.

artificialism: A belief that all living animate and inanimate things are made, usually by humans, in the same way.

assimilation: According to Jean Piaget, the manner in which a child responds to new experiences through the use of existing concepts to interpret new experiences.

attachment: According to Erik Erikson, the bond between a child and his or her parents or caregivers.

autonomy (versus shame and doubt): According to Erik Erikson, the psychosocial crisis of children in the struggle to control their own thoughts, feelings, and action (age usually 9–18 months).

babbling: The production of syllables containing vowel and consonant sounds made by prespeech infants for the purpose of play and communication with the caregiver.

basic trust vs. mistrust: According to Erik Erikson, the psychosocial struggle by children to develop a sense of trust in the caregiver (usually neonatal through 9 months).

behavior modification: An empirical procedure designed to change behavior through the use of positive and/or negative reinforcement.

behaviorism: An empirical learning theory that observes and records behaviors as an indication of what has been learned.

canalization: The theory that an organism tends to return to its hereditarily determined path of development after being pushed off that path by a temporary disturbance.

castration anxiety: According to Sigmund Freud, fear by a male child that he will be punished by his father by castration for desiring to possess his mother exclusively.

centration: According to Piaget, a young child's inclination to focus attention on one element of a task or one dimension of an object.

chaining: The linking together of already learned units into the proper sequence.

cognition: The process that enables individuals to acquire knowledge.

cognitive style: Contrasting patterns of perception that exist among individuals during the learning process.

concrete operational stage: According to Jean Piaget, the developmental period when children can use logic, understand relationships among concepts, and think abstractly (approximately 6–9 years of age).

conditioned response: According to Ivan Pavlov, a learned behavior that can be elicited by a conditioned stimulus through an association with an unconditioned stimulus.

conscience: According to Freud, the punitive side of norms identified by the superego, telling the individual what must be done, and calling up guilt if the suggestion is not followed.

conservation: The knowledge that certain properties remain constant in volume and quantity, for example, despite changes in dimensions like shape and position.

construction of knowledge: According to Jean Piaget, the process by which a child creates a mental explanation for experiences.

constructivist: According to Piaget, children construct their knowledge of the world and create cognitive structures through their activity.

critical period: Sometimes referred to as a *sensitive period,* a period during which a part of the organism is affected by environmental influences that have an insignificant effect at other times.

decentration: According to Jean Piaget, a broadening of attention that occurs as children develop concrete operations, and learn to pay attention to more than one element of a task or more than one dimension of an object.

defense mechanism: According to Sigmund Freud, a subconscious (erroneously labeled "unconscious" by Freud) process through which an individual reduces anxiety by distorting or repressing reality to reduce anxiety.

deferred imitation: According to Jean Piaget, the capacity of a child ages two to seven to imitate a behavior at a later time beyond when it was first witnessed.

development: Long-term changes in a individual's thoughts, feelings, relationships, motor skills/coordination, and thinking.

developmental stages: Stages that mark the process of change in individuals. All individuals share age-related features that are sequenced by stages of development. Each stage represents a logical progression in development and is significantly different from the previous stage and the stage that follows.

disequilibrium: According to Jean Piaget, this is a temporary cognitive state in which new information cannot be integrated or reconciled with existing information or experiences.

divergent thinking: The capacity to generate a variety of ideas that are associated with each other in unusual ways.

Down syndrome: A genetic deviation in which an individual has an extra 21st chromosome accompanied by some degree of mental abnormality and physical features common to this group of children.

dyslexia: A common disability involving difficulties in reading.

early-childhood education: A period of public and/or private education for children ages birth through eight.

ecological view: The identification of psychological problems, and a view of developmental changes, being caused or influenced by layers of social influences like family, occupation, and friendship issues.

ego: According to Sigmund Freud, that aspect of personality that seeks to resolve conflicts that arise between drives (hunger, sex, etc.) and reality.

egocentrism: According to Sigmund Freud, our behavior and thoughts are self-centered and we are unable to recognize another person's point of view.

empathy: Identifying with another person's emotional state, when in your view it could be similar to your own emotional state, i.e., feeling distress when another person is in distress.

equilibration: According to Jean Piaget, the stage at which an individual's thinking becomes stable and in harmony with the environment.

ethology: A field of study that gives special attention to the examination of the organism's behavior in its natural environment.

exosystem: According to Urie Bronfenbrenner, parts of the environment that children do not enter but that affect them nonetheless.

formal operation: According to Jean Piaget, the fourth stage of cognitive development starting at approximately age 12 and extending through adulthood, gender: The social implications of being male or female.

id: According to Sigmund Freud, that aspect of personality that seeks the immediate gratification of basic drives.

infant: A baby from birth to 12 months of age (see also *toddler*).

internalization: According to Sigmund Freud, the acquisition into a person's own personality of important qualities of the same-gender parent, and a phase in the child's negotiation of the Oedipal conflict, including the act of holding in feelings.

K–12: The public or private education of children starting in kindergarten and continuing through grade 12.

latency: According to Sigmund Freud, the stage of development that follows the phallic stage, when sexual feelings are temporarily sequestered as the child attempts to resolve Oedipal conflicts.

libido: According to Sigmund Freud, the many ways that individuals seek to increase pleasures and avoid displeasure, usually by fulfilling emotional and physical needs.

macrosystem: According to Urie Bronfenbrenner, the most global level of the environment that describes the consistencies in lower-level systems across a society or mesosystem; the level of the environment that includes culture.

mesosystem: According to Urie Bronfenbrenner, the level of the environment that reflects the connections between a child's home and school.

Moro reflex: A reflex elicited by placing infants on their backs and abruptly reducing support. In response it is expected that the infants will arch their back, extend their legs, throw their arms outward, then pull them back toward each other.

neonate: A newborn infant during the first four to six weeks of life.

object permanence: According to Jean Piaget, during the first 24 months of life, children do not believe that persons and things exist when they cannot be experienced directly.

Oedipal conflict: According to Sigmund Freud, the phallic stage emerges in male children when a desire for the parent of the opposite gender and the accompanying disappointment at the realization that the same-gender parent will win the competition for this parent.

operant conditioning: According to B.F. Skinner, a type of knowledge that occurs when future behaviors are controlled through repeated reinforcement of that behavior.

oral stage: According to Sigmund Freud, the stage of development during the first year of life, in which the id is dominant and where the infant seeks satisfaction of emotional and physical drives through the mouth.

penis envy: According to Sigmund Freud, a four- or five-year-old girl's desire for a penis that results in an envy of its ownership by boys.

perception: The combining of sensations into meaningful patterns through neuronal activity.

preoperational: According to Jean Piaget, the stage of cognitive development starting around 18 months and extending to age six, during which time children acquire knowledge through perceptions and experiences.

preschooler: A child three to five years of age.

preterm: An infant born before the 36th week after fertilization.

psychoanalysis: A treatment process devised by Sigmund Freud for the treatment of persons who are mentally ill or think that they are. This treatment encourages patients to talk over extended periods of time, usually without interruption, about recollections of past experiences and how current thoughts interact with past experiences.

psychosexual stage: According to Sigmund Freud, the psychological consequences of changes during early sexuality during the phase of development that reflect changes in sexual energy on different bodily organs along with changes in behavior.

psychosocial stage: According to Erik Erikson, phases of development that are consequences of particularized events during the life cycle.

rooting reflex: An infant's response to a touch on the cheek. The response includes turning the head toward the object, opening the mouth, and closing in on the object.

scaffolding: According to Lev Vygotsky, the assistance a peer or adult provides a child in acquiring knowledge or developing a skill.

sensorimotor: According to Jean Piaget, the stage of cognitive development starting at birth and extending through 18 months of age, during which time children's growth in thinking is governed primarily by what they perceive through their senses and reflex movements.

sex: The biological implications of being male or female.

sickle-cell anemia: A genetically transmitted human condition in which a person's red blood cells acquire a curved, sickle shape and clog circulation in the small blood vessels. Found primarily among persons of African descent.

social learning theory: A theory that learning results from observations and interactions with others.

stage theory: A theory that proposes steps in a fixed sequence that form a logical hierarchy in growth and development when compared to one another.

superego: According to Sigmund Freud, the aspect of personality that acts to demonstrate the expectations and norms of a culture.

symbiotic mother-child relationships: According to Margaret Mahler, a characteristic of the mother's first year in which the mother conceptualizes the child as an extension of herself and the child has a similar perception.

Tay-Sachs disease: A genetically transmitted disorder of the nervous system that occurs mainly among Jewish infants with parents of Eastern European decent.

toddler: A baby from 12 to 18 months of age (see also *infant*).

trisomy: The chromosomal abnormality that most often causes Down syndrome, which is the presence of three rather than the normal two chromosomes of type 21.

Turner syndrome: A sex chromosome abnormality that results from the presence of only one chromosome, an X. Children with this abnormality are often sterile and have low visual-spatial abilities.

withdrawal reflex: A newborn's tendency to flex the knee and move the foot away if he or she feels a pinprick on the bottom of one foot.

zone of proximal development: According to Lev Vygotsky, the difference between the level of cognitive development that children display when working independently and the level they display when working with a more capable assistant.

Bibliography

Acredolo, L., and S. Goodwyn. 1988. Symbolic gesturing in normal infants. *Child Development.* 59: 450–466.

Acredolo, L., and S. Goodwyn. 1998. *Baby signs.* Chicago: Contemporary Books.

Adamson, L. B., and R. Bakeman. 1984. Mother's communicative acts: Changes during infancy. *Infant Behavior and Development.* 7: 467–478.

Addams, J. 1910. *Twenty years at Hull-House.* New York: Macmillan.

Addams, J. 1964. *Democracy and social ethics.* Cambridge, MA: Harvard University Press.

Ainsworth, M. D. 1962. The effects of maternal deprivation: A review of findings and controversy in the context of research strategy. In *Deprivation of maternal care: A reassessment of its effects.* Geneva, Switzerland: World Health Organization.

Ainsworth, M. D. and S. M. Bell. 1970. Attachment, exploration, and separation: Illustrated by the behavior of one-year-olds in a strange situation. *Child Development.* 41: 49–67.

Ainsworth, M., M. C. Blehar, E. Waters, and S. Wall. 1978. *Patterns of attachment: A psychological study of the strange situation.* Hillsdale, NJ: Erlbaum.

Anisfield, M. 1984. *Language development from birth to three.* Hillsdale, NJ: Erlbaum.

Aries, P. 1962. *Centuries of childhood: A social history of family life,* trans. Robert Baldick. New York: Alfred A. Knopf.

Armbruster, B. B. 2003. *A child becomes a reader: Kindergarten to grade 3.* Washington, DC: National Institute for Literacy.

Associated Press Wire Service. 2004 (April 22). *Boy, 8, who brought gun to school was bullied, neighbors say.*

Atkinson, K. B., B. MacWhinney, and C. Stoel. 1970. An experiment in the recognition of babbling. *Papers and Reports in Child Language Development.* 5: 1–8.

Bach, G. F. 1946. Father fantasies and father typing in father separated children. *Child Development.* 17. 63–80.

Bachmann, M. 1991. *Dalcroze today: An education through and into music*. Oxford: Clarendon Press.

Bailey, J. M., and R. C. Pillard. 1991. A genetic study of male sexual orientation. *Archives of General Psychiatry*. 43: 808–812.

Baillargeon, R., and J. DeVos. 1991. Object permanence in young infants. Further evidence. *Child Development*. 62: 1227–1246.

Bakeman, R., and L. B. Adamson. 1984. Coordinating attention to people and objects in mother-infant and peer infant interaction. *Child Development*. 55: 1278–1289.

Balderrama, F. E., and R. Rodriquez. 1995. *Decade of betrayal: Mexican reparation in the 1930s*. Albuquerque, NM: University of New Mexico Press.

Baldwin, J. M. 1897. *Social and ethnic interpretations in mental development: A study in social psychology*. New York: Macmillan.

Bandura, A. L. 1977. *Social learning theory*. Englewood Cliffs, NJ: Prentice Hall.

Bandura, A. L. 1986. *Social foundations of thought and action*. Englewood Cliffs, NJ: Prentice Hall.

Bandura, A. L. 1991. Social cognitive theory of moral thought and action. In *Handbook of moral behavior and development, vol. 1*, ed. W. M. Kurtines and J. L. Gerwitz, 45–103. Hilldale, NJ: Erlbaum.

Barnett, S. W., J. T. Hustedt, K. B. Robbin, and K. L. Schulman. 2004. *The state of preschool*. New Brunswick, NJ: The National Institute for Early Education Research.

Barnouw, E. 1970. *Adventures with children in nursery school and kindergarten*. New York: Agathon Press.

Barrera, M. E., and D. Maurer. 1981. Recognition of mother's photographed face by a three-month-old. *Child Development*. 52: 714–716.

Baumrind, D. 1967. Child-care practices anteceding three patterns of preschool behavior. *Genetic Psychology Monographs*. 75: 43–88.

Baumrind, D. 1986. Sex differences in moral reasoning: Response to Walker's conclusion that there are none. *Child Development*. 57: 511–521.

Baylor, R. M. 1965. *Elizabeth Peabody: Kindergarten pioneer*. Philadelphia: University of Pennsylvania Press.

Beaty, Janice J. 2005. *50 early childhood literacy strategies*. Upper Saddle River, NJ: Pearson, Merrill, Prentice Hall.

Beecher, C. 1851. *The true remedy for the wrongs of women*. Boston: Sampson.

Beecher, C. 1856. *Common sense applied to religion, or the Bible and the people*. New York: Harper and Brothers.

Beecher, C. 1871. *Woman suffrage and woman's profession*. Hartford, CT: Brown and Gross.

Beecher, C. 1874. *Educational reminiscences and suggestions*. New York: J. B. Ford.

Beilin, H. 1992. Piaget's enduring contribution to developmental psychology. *Developmental Psychology*. 28: 191–204.

Bell, A., M. Weinberg, and S. Hammersmith. 1981. *Sexual preference: Its development in men and women*. Bloomington, IN: Indiana University Press.

Belsky, J., B. Gilstrap, and M. Rovine. 1984. The Pennsylvania infant and family project, I: Stability and change in mother-infant and father-infant setting at one, two, three, and 9 months. *Child Development*. 55: 692–705.

Belsky, J., M. Rovine, and D. G. Taylor. 1984. The Pennsylvania infant and family project, III: The origins of individual differences in infant-mother attachment: Maternal and infant contributions. *Child Development.* 55: 718–728.

Bernal, M. 1987. *Black Athena: The Afroasiatic roots of classical civilization.* New Brunswick, NJ: Rutgers University Press.

Bernstein, B. 1961. Social class and linguistic development: A theory of social learning. In *Economy, education, and society,* ed. A. H. Halsey, J. Floud, and C. A. Anderson. New York: Free Press.

Berrueta-Clement, J. R., L. J. Schweinhart, S. W. Barnett, A. S. Epstein, and D. P. Weikart. 1984. *Changed lives: The effects of the Perry Preschool Program on the youths through age 19.* Ypsilanti, MI: High Scope/Educational Research Foundation, No. 8.

Bolby, J. 1969. *Attachment.* New York: Basic Books.

Boyd, W. 1911. *The educational theory of Jean-Jacques Rousseau.* London: Longmans, Green and Company.

Brazelton, T. B. 1973. Neonatal behavioral assessment scale. *Clinics in Developmental Medicine,* No. 50. Philadelphia, PA: Lippincott.

Brodal, P. 1998. *The central nervous system: Structure and function.* New York: Oxford University Press.

Bronfenbrenner, U. 1979. *The ecology of human development.* MA: Harvard University Press.

Bronfenbrenner, U. 1986. Ecology of the family in a context for human development: Research perspectives. *Developmental Psychology.* 22: 723–742.

Brooks-Gunn, J., P. K. Klebanov, and G. J. Duncan. 1996. Ethnic differences in children's intelligence test scores: Role of economic deprivation, home environment, and maternal characteristics. *Child Development.* 67: 396–408.

Brooks-Gunn, J., and W. S. Matthews. 1979. *He and she: How children develop their sex role identity.* Englewood Cliffs, NJ: Prentice Hall.

Cairns, R. 1979. *Social development: The origins of plasticity of interchanges.* San Francisco: Freeman.

Caldwell, B. J. 2005. The new interprise logic of schools. *Phi Delta Kappan.* 87 (November): 23–25.

Calvert, K. L. F. 1992. *Children in the house: The material culture of early childhood, 1600–1900.* Boston, MA: Northeastern University Press.

Carr, Margaret. 2001. *Assessment in early childhood settings: Learning stories.* London: P. Chapman Publishing.

Chall, J. S. 1983. *Learning to read: The great debate.* New York: McGraw Hill.

Chall, J. S. 1987. Reading and early childhood education: The critical issues. *Principal.* 66(5).

Chall, J. S. 1990. *The reading crisis: Why poor children fall behind.* Cambridge, MA: Harvard University Press.

Chall, J. S. 2000. *The reading achievement challenge: What really works in the classroom.* New York: Guilford Press.

Chattin-McNichols, J. 1992. *The Montessori controversy.* Albany, NY: Delmar.

Cohen, R. M., and Scheer, S. 1997. *The work of teachers in America.* Mahwah, NJ: Lawrence Erlbaum Associates.

Cole, L. 1950. *A history of education: Socrates to Montessori*. New York: Holt, Rinehart and Winston.

Cole, M. I. 1953. *Robert Owen of New Lanark*. London: Batchworth Press.

Comenius, J. A. (1659) (*The visible world*), Orbus Sensualism Pictus, trans. Charles Hoole. London, UK: J. Kirton.

Comenius, J. A. 1901. *The school of infancy*, ed. Will S. Monroe. Boston: D. C. Heath and Company.

Comenius, J. A. 1957. *John Amos Comenius on education*. With an introduction by Jean Piaget. New York: Teachers College Press.

Comenius, J. A. 1998. The labyrinth of the world and the paradise of the heart. trans. Howard Louthan and Andrea Sterk. Paulist Press, New York.

Cook, M., and J. Cohen. 1990. How television sold the Panama invasion. *Fairness and Accurcy in Reporting (FAIR)*. (February).

Darling-Hammond, L. 2005. Teaching as a profession: Lessons in teacher preparation and professional development. *Phi Delta Kappan*. 87 (November): 237–240.

Dewey, J. 1899. *The school and society*. Chicago: Universiy of Chicago Press.

Dewey, J. 1902. *The child and the curriculum*. Chicago: University of Chicago Press.

Dewey, J. 1916. *Democracy and education*. New York: Macmillan.

Dewey, J. 1933. *How we think*. Lexington, MA: D. C. Heath.

Dewey, J. 1938. *Experience and education*. Chicago: University of Chicago Press.

Doe, C. 1990. Circle tales deluxe: Interactive nursery rhymes for young learners. *Multi Media Schools*. 6: 59–60.

Dinges, J. 1991. *Our man in Panama: The shrewd rise and brutal fall of Manuel Noriega*. New York: Random House.

Dunst, C. J. 1980. *A clinical and educational manual for use with the Usgiris and Hunt scales of infant psychological development*. Baltimore: University Park Press.

Early education and care: Overlap indicates need to assess cross cutting programs. 2000. Washington, D.C.: U. S. General Accounting Office, No. GAO/ HEHS-00-78.

Eco, U. 2004. *Umberto Eco on literature*. New York: Harcourt, Inc.

Edelson, K., and R. C. Orem. 1970. *The Children's House parent-teacher guide to Montessori*. New York: Putnam.

Eisenberg, A., H. Murkoff, and S. Hathaway. 1989. *What to expect the first year*. New York: Workman.

Eller, E. M. 1956. *The school of infancy*. Chapel Hill: University of North Carolina.

Erikson, E. 1950. *Childhood and society*. New York: Norton.

Fabian, H., and A. W. Dunlop, eds. 2002. *Transitions in the early years: Debating continuity and progression for children in early education*. London: Routledge Falmer.

Fagan, J. F., and S. K. McGrath. 1981. Infant recognition memory and later intelligence. *Intelligence*. 5: 121–130.

Fernald, A. 1985. Four-month-old infants prefer to listen to motherese. *Infant Behavior and Development*. 8: 181–195.

Findlay, E. 1971. *Rhythm and movement: Application of Delcroze eurhythmics*. Evanston, IL: Summy Brichard.

Fisher, Dorothy C. 1913. *The Montessori manual for teachers and parents*. Cambridge, MA: R. Bentley.

Fleming, G. A. 1954. *Creative rhythmic movement for children*. New York: Prentice-Hall.

Forward, S. and C. Buck. 1979. *Betrayal of innocence*. New York: Penguin Books.

Franzen, J. 1996. Perchance a dream. *Harper's* (April).

Freud, S. 1954. *The origins of psychoanalysis*. New York: Basic Books.

Freud, S. 1961. *Some psychological consequences of the anatomical distinction between the sexes.* In *Standard edition of the complete psychological works of Sigmund Freud*, ed. J. C. Strachey. London: Hogarth Press.

Freud, S. 1965. *Group psychology and the analysis of the ego*. New York: Bantam Books.

Froebel, F. 1887. *The education of man*. New York: D. Appleton and Co.

Froebel, F. 1900. *Pedagogies of kindergarten,* trans. Josephine Jarvis. London: Edward Arnold and Company.

Gay, P. 1988. *Freud: A life for our time*. New York: W. W. Norton.

Gesell, A., and C. Amatruda. 1941. *Developmental diagnosis*. New York: Paul B. Hoeber.

Giel, K. 1959. *Fichte and Froebel*. Heidelberg: Quelle and Meyer.

Gilboa, E. 1995. The Panama invasion revisited: Lessons for the use of force in the post Cold War era. *Political Science Quarterly.* 110: 539–550.

Ginsburg, H., and S. Opper. 1969. *Piaget's theory of intellectual development: An introduction*. Englewood Cliffs, NJ: Prentice Hall.

Giroux, H. A. 1981. *Curriculum and instruction: Alternatives in education.* Berkeley, CA: McCutchan Publishing Corporation.

Giroux, H. A., A. N. Penna, and W. E. Pinar. 1981. *Curriculum and instruction: Alternatives in education*. Berkeley, CA: McCutchan Publishing Corporation.

Glenn, S. M. and Cunningham, C. C. 1984. Nursery rhymes and early language acquisition by mentally handicapped children. *Exceptional Children.* 51: 72–74.

Goodenough, F. L. 1928. *The Kuhlman-Binet tests for children of preschool age*. Minneapolis: The University of Minnesota Press.

Goodenough, F. L. 1928a. A preliminary report on the effects of nursery school training upon intelligence test scores of young children. *27th Yearbook of the National Society of Education,* 361–369.

Goodenough, F. L. 1939. Look to the evidence: A critique of recent experiments on raising the IQ. *Education Methods.* 19: 73–79.

Graves, K. 1998. *Girls' schooling during the Progressive Era*. New York: Garland Publishing.

Green, F. C. 1955. *Jean-Jacques Rousseau: A study of his life and writings*. Cambridge: Cambridge University Press.

Green, J. A. 1913. *Life and work of Pestalozzi*. London: University Tutorial Press.

Green, J. A. 1969. *The educational ideas of Pestalozzi*. New York: Greenwood Press.

Gromley, W. T. 2005. The universal pre-K bandwagon. *Phi Delta Kappan.* 87: 246–249.

Guarino, D. 1997. *Is your mama a llama?* New York: Scholastic.

Hacker, A. 1994. White on white. *The New Republic.* October 31.

Hainstook, Elizabeth G. 1968. *Teaching Montessori in the home: The pre school years*. New York: New American Library.

Hainstock, Elizabeth G. 1986. *The essential Montessori.* New York: New American Library.

Harvey, K. D., L. D. Harjo, and J. K. Jackson. 1997. *Teaching about Native Americans.* Washington, DC: National Council for the Social Studies.

Heafford, Michael R. 1967. *Pestalozzi: His thought and its relevance today.* London: Methuen and Co. Ltd.

Hechinger, P. 1979. Further proof that I.Q. data were fraudulent. *The New York Times.* (December 28).

Hecht, P. 2005. Mass eviction in Mexico in 1930s spurs apology. *The Sacramento Bee.* February 10.

Herrenkohl, R. C., and J. M. Russo. 2001. *Child maltreatment.* Thousand Oaks, CA: Sage.

Hershfield, V. D. 2004. Second-grader suspended for bringing gun to school. *Union Leader.* February 10.

Hill, R. L. 2005. Police: 5-year-old took gun to school; Fifth grader is credited with taking away loaded weapon, turning it in. *Austin American-Statesman.* May 18.

Hixon, D. 1982. *A curriculum guide for teaching black history to kindergarten and first grade students.* Ed.D. thesis, West Georgia College, Carrollton, GA.

Hohmann, M., and D. P. Weikart. 1995. *Educating young children.* Ypsilanti, MI: High/Scope Press.

Hunt, J. M. 1961. *Intelligence and experience.* New York: Wiley.

Hymes, James L. 1978–1979. *Early childhood education: Living history interviews.* Carmel, CA: Hacienda Press.

Jacobson, Tamar. 2003. *Confronting our discomfort: Clearing the way for anti-bias in early childhood.* Portsmouth, NH: Heinemann.

Johnson, O. C. 1970. *Robert Owen in the United States.* New York: Humanities Press.

Jones, Lloyd. 1971. *The life, times, and labours of Robert Owen.* New York: AMS Press.

Jones, R. M. 1970. *Fantasy and feeling in education.* New York: New York University Press.

Jusczyk, P. W. 1997. *The discovery of spoken language.* Cambridge, MA: MIT Press.

Kagan, J. 1984. *The nature of the child.* New York: Basic Books.

Kagan, S. L., P. R. Britto, and P. Engle. 2005. Early learning standards: What can America learn? What can American teach? *Phi Delta Kappan* 87 (November).

Kagan, S. L., and V. Stewart. 2005. A new world view: Education in a global era. *Phi Delta Kappan.* 87 (November). 185–187.

Kamerman, S. B. 2005. Early childhood and care in advanced industrialized countries: Current policy trends. *Phi Delta Kappan.* 87 (November). 193–195.

Kamii, C. 1976. *Piaget, children, and number: Applying Piaget's theory to the teaching of elementary number.* Washington, DC: National Association for the Education of Young Children.

Kamii, C. 1989. *Young children continue to reinvent arithmetic—2nd grade: Implications of Piaget's theory.* New York: Teachers College Press.

Kamii, C., and G. DeClark. 1985. *Young children reinvent arithmetic: Implications for Piaget's theory.* New York: Teachers College Press.

Kamin, L. 1974. *The science and politics of IQ.* Potomac, MD: Lawrence Erlbaum.

Katz, L., and S. C. Chard. 1989. *Engaging children's minds: The project approach.* Greenwich, CT: Ablex Publication Corp.

Kilpatrick, W. H. 1916. *Froebel's kindergarten principles.* New York: The Macmillan Company.

Kilpatrick, W. H. 1918. The project method. *Teacher's College Record.* 24 (September): 319–325.

Kilpatrick, W. H. 1926. *Foundations of education.* New York: Macmillan.

Kincheloe, J.L., and W. F. Pinar. 1991. *Curriculum as social psychoanalysis: The significance of place.* Albany: State University of New York Press.

Kirsch, I. 2002. *Reading for change: Performance and engagement across countries: Results from PISA 2000.* Paris: OECD.

Knobloch, H., and B. Pasamanick. 1974. *Gesell and Amatruda's developmental diagnosis.* New York: Harper and Row.

Knobloch, H., F. Stevens, and A. Malone. 1980. *The manual of developmental diagnosis.* New York: Harper and Row.

Kopp, C. 1994. *Baby steps.* New York: W. H. Freeman.

Kramer, R. 1976. *Maria Montessori: A biography.* New York: Putnam.

Labov, W. 2000. *Principles of linguistic change, Volume 2: Social factors.* Malden, MA: Blackwell Publishers.

Lancaster, J. 1821. *The Lancastrian system of education improvements.* Baltimore, MD: Joseph Lancaster.

Laurendeau, M., and A. Pinard. 1970. *The development of the concept of space in the child.* New York: International Universities Press, Inc.

Lawrence, E. M. 1969. *Froebel and English education: Perspectives on the founder of the kindergarten.* New York: Schocken Books.

Leik, R., and M. Chalkley. 1990. Parent involvement: What is it that works? *Children Today.* 19: 34–37.

Leonard, L. B., M. Newhoff, and L. Mesalam. 1980. Individual differences in early childhood phonology. *Applied Psycholinguistics.* 1: 7–30.

Leopold, Richard W. 1940. *Robert Dale Owen, a biography.* New York: Octagon Books.

Levine, H. L. 2005. Take a giant step: Investing in preschool education in emerging nations. *Phi Delta Kappan.* 87:162–200.

Lewis, M. 1973. Intelligence tests: Their use and misuse. *Human Development.* 17: 108–118.

Lewis, M. 1983. *Origins of intelligence: Infancy and early childhood.* New York: Plenum Press.

Lewis, M., and L. A. Rosenblum. 1974. The *effects of the infant on its caregiver.* New York: Wiley.

Liaw, F., S. J. Meisels, and J. Brooks-Gunn, J. 1995. The effects of experience of early intervention on low birth weight, premature children: The infant health and development program. *Early Childhood Quarterly.* 10: 405.

Liben, L. S., M. Moore, M., and S. Golbeck. 1982. Preschoolers knowledge of their classroom environment: Evidence from small-scale and life-size spatial tasks. *Child Development* 53 (5): 1275–1284.

150

Bibliography

Liebschner, J. 2001. *A child's work: Freedom and practice in Froebel's educational theory and practice.* Cambridge: Lutterworth.

Lilley, I. M., ed. 1967. *Friedrich Froebel: A selection of his writings by Irene M. Lilley.* Cambridge, UK: Cambridge University Press.

Lippman, W. 1995. A future for the test. In *The bell curve* ed. R. Jacoby and N. Glauberman, 566–582. New York: Random House.

Lipsitt, L., and H. Kaye. 1964. Conditioned sucking in the newborn. *Psychonomic Science.* 1: 29–30.

Locke, J. L. 1968. *The educational writings: A critical edition,* ed J. L. Axtell. Cambridge: Cambridge University Press.

Locke, J. L. 1983. *Phonological acquisition and change.* New York: Academic Press.

Locke, J. L. 1993. *A child's path to spoken language.* Cambridge, MA: Harvard University Press.

Loeffler, Howard. 1992. *Montessori in contemporary American culture.* Portsmouth, NH: Heinemann.

Luban, David. 2005. Torture, American-style: This debate comes down to words vs. deeds. *Washington Post.* November 27, B01.

Lundberg, I. 1999. Learning to read in Scandinavia. In *Learning to read and write: Cross-linguistic perspective,* ed. Margaret Harris and Giyoo Hatano. Cambridge: Cambridge University Press.

Macleod, D. I. 1998. *The age of the child: Children in America, 1890–1920.* New York: Twayne.

MacWhinney, B. 1998. *The emergence of language.* Hillsdale, NJ: Erlbaum.

Mallory, N., and Goldsmith, N. 1990. Head Start works! Two Head Start veterans share their views. *Young Children.* 45 (6): 36–39.

Marshall, M. 1987. *Three sisters who showed the way.* New York: American Heritage.

Martin, A. 1985. Back to kindergarten basics. *Harvard Educational Review.* 55 (3): 318–320.

Maslow, A. 1968. *Goals of humanistic education.* Big Sur, CA: Esalen Institute.

Masson, J. M. 1985. *The complete letters of Sigmund Freud to William Fliess, 1887–1904.* Cambridge, MA: The Belknap Press.

Matlin, M. W. 1993. *The psychology of women.* Fort Worth, TX: Harcourt Brace.

Maurer, D., and C. Maurer. 1988. *The world of the newborn.* New York: Basic Books.

McDonald, R. 2005. Thirteen-year-old charged with felony; Mead student brought gun to school, stashed it in boys' restroom. *Spokesman Review.* January 13.

McGee, L. M. 2003. *Designing early literacy programs: Strategies for at-risk preschool and kindergarten children.* New York: Guilford Press.

Messinger, D. S., and A. Fogel. 1998. Give and take: The development of conventional infant gestures. *Merrill-Palmer Quarterly.* 44: 566–590.

Montessori, M. M. 1976. *Education for human development: Understanding Montessori.* New York: Schocken Books.

Morgan, H. 1973. *The learning community.* Columbus, OH: Charles Merrill.

Morgan, H. 1997. *Cognitive styles and classroom learning.* Westport, CT: Praeger Publishers.

Morgan, H. 1999. *The imagination of early childhood education.* Westport, CT: Bergin and Garvey.

Morgan, H. 2003. *Real learning: A bridge to cognitive neuroscience.* Lanham, MD: Rowman and Littlefield.

Mosier, C. E., and B. Rogoff. 1994. Infant's instrumental use of their mothers to achieve their goals. *Child Development.* 65: 70–79.

Murguia, E. 1975. *Assimilation, colonialism and the Mexican American people.* Austin, TX: University of Texas Press.

Murphy, D. J. 1996. *Comenius: A critical reassessment of his life and work.* Dublin: Irish Academic Press.

Naylor, P. C. 2000. *France and Algeria: A history of decolonization and transformation.* Gainesville, FL: The University of Florida Press.

Neuman, M. J. 2005. Global care and education: Challenges, responses, and lessons. *Phi Delta Kappan*, 87 (3) 188–192.

New, R. S. (2005). Learning about early childhood education from and with Western European Nations. *Phi Delta Kappan.* 87 (3): 201–204s.

Niemeyer, J. A. 2002. *Assessing kindergarten children: A compendium of assessment instruments.* Chapel Hill, NC: University of North Carolina Press.

Orem, R. C. 1974. *Montessori: Her method and the movement.* New York: G. P. Putnam's Sons.

Orem, Reginald C. 1969. *Montessori and the special child.* New York: Putnam.

Osofsky, J. 1987. *Handbook of infant development.* New York: Wiley.

Owen, R. 1838. *The marriage system of the new moral world.* Leeds, UK: J. Hobson.

Owen, R. 1920. *Life of Robert Owen: Written by himself.* London: G. Bell and Sons.

Owen, R. 1969. *Robert Owen on education.* London: Cambridge University Press.

Owen, R. 1970. *Robert Owen in the United States.* New York: Humanities Press.

Palmer, J. A. 2001. *Fifty major thinkers on education: From Confucius to Dewey.* New York: Routledge.

Parkerson, D. H., and J. A. Parkerson. 2001. *Traditions in American education.* New York: Routledge Farmer.

Pavlov, I. P. 1927. *Conditioned reflexes: An investigation of the physiological activity of the cerebral cortex*, trans. G. V. Anrep. London: Oxford University Press.

Pestalozzi, J. H. 1885. *Leonard and Gertrude.* London: D. C. Heath and Company.

Pestalozzi, J. H. 1907. *How Gertrude teaches her children.* London: Swan Sonnenschein and Company, Ltd.

Piaget, J. 1952. *The origin of intelligence in children.* New York: International Universities Press.

Piaget, J. 1954. *The construction of reality in the child.* New York: Free Press.

Pinard, W. F. 1975. *Curriculum theorizing: The reconceptualists.* Berkeley, CA: McCutchan Publishing Corporation.

Pinard, W. F. 1998. *Curriculum: Toward new identities.* New York: Garland Publishing Company.

Pinard, W. F. 1999. *Contemporary curriculum discourses: Twenty years of JCT.* New York: P. Lang.

Pinard, W. F. 2003. *International handbook of curriculum research.* Mahwah, NJ: L. Erlbaum Associates.

Pizzo, P. 1990. Family-centered Head Start for infants and toddlers. A renewed direction for project Head Start. *Young Children.* 45 (6): 30–35.

Polanyi, M. 1969. *Knowing and being.* Chicago, Ill: The University of Chicago Press.

Powers, W. T. 1973. *Behavior: The control of perception.* Chicago: Aldine Publishing Company.

Prechtl, H., and D. Beintema. 1964. *The neurological examination of the full term newborn infant.* London: Heinemann.

Randall, J. A. 1915. Project teaching. *National Education Association.* 1009–1012.

Reeder, E. 2005. *Measuring what counts: Memorization versus understanding.* Edutopia Online, http://www.glef.org.

Rensberger, R. 1976. Briton's classic I.Q. data now viewed as fraudulent. *The New York Times.* November 28.

Richter, A. 1937. *Ada Richter's kindergarten class book, a piano for little tots, using* Goldilocks and the Three Bears *as a foundation story.* Philadelphia: Theodore Presser Co.

Robinson, J. 1921. A project in community life in the kindergarten. *Elementary School Journal.* 22: 194–203.

Rogers, C. 1969. Freedom to learn. Columbus, OH: Charles Merrill.

Rogoff, B., and J. V. Wertsch. (1984). *Children's learning in the "zone of proximal development."* San Francisco: Jossey-Bass.

Ronda, B. 1999. *Elizabeth Palmer Peabody: A reformer on her own terms.* Cambridge, MA: Harvard University Press.

Rosenblith, J. F. 1961. *Manual for behavioral examination of the neonate as modified by Rosenblith from Graham.* Providence, RI: Brown Duplicating Service.

Rousseau, J. 1762; 1911. *Emile, or, On education.* London: Dent.

Rousseau, J. 1964. *Emile, Julie, and other writings,* ed. S. E. Frost, Jr., trans. R. L. Archer. Woodbury, NY: Barron's Educational Series.

Rugoff, M. 1981. *The Beechers: An American family in the nineteenth century.* New York: Harper and Row.

Rusk, R. R. 1967. *A history of infant education.* London: University of London Press.

Rust, F. O. 1993. *Changing teaching, changing schools: Bringing early childhood practice into public education: Case studies from kindergarten.* New York: Teachers College Press.

Ryan, S. (1993). The Panama deception. *Cineaste.* 20 (Winter): 43.

Sadler, J. E. 1966. *J. A. Comenius and the concept of universal education.* London: Allen and Unwin.

Salot, L. 1965. *The beginning kindergarten teacher.* Minneapolis: Burgess Publishing Company.

Sameroff, A., and P. Cavanaugh. 1979. Learning in infancy: A developmental perspective. In *Handbook of infant development,* ed. J. Osofosky. New York: Wiley.

Schickedanz, J. A. 1997. *Curriculum in early childhood: A resource guide for preschoolers and kindergarten teachers.* Boston: Allyn and Bacon.

Sears, R. 2005. Quince student has hit list, girl tells cop; he allegedly wrote bomb threat, brought gun to school; accused of planting grenade plead innocent. *The Patriotic Ledger.* February 16.

Shapiro, M. S. 1983. *Child's garden: The kindergarten movement from Froebel to Dewey.* University Park: Pennsylvania State University Press.

Silber, K. 1960. *The man and his work.* London: Routledge and Kegan Paul.

Silver, H. 1969. *Robert Owen on education.* Cambridge: Cambridge University Press.

Simpson, B. R. 1939. The wandering IQ: Is it time to settle down? *Journal of Psychology.* 7: 351–367.

Skinner, B. F. 1938. *The behavior of organisms: An experimental analysis.* New York: Appleton-Century-Crofts.

Skinner, B. F. 1953. *Science of human behavior.* New York: Macmillian.

Skinner, B. F. 1957. *Verbal behavior.* New York: Appleton-Century-Crofts.

Sklar, K. K. 1973. *Catherine Beecher: A study in domesticity.* New Haven, CT: Yale University Press.

Skodak, M. 1939. Children in foster homes: A study of mental development. *University of Iowa Studies in Child Welfare.* 16: 1.

Snedden, D. 1916. The project as a teaching unit. *School and Society.* 4 (September): 419–423.

Snyder, Agnes. 1972. *Dauntless women in childhood education, 1856–1931.* Washington, DC: Association for Childhood Education International.

Somerville, S. C., and P. E. Bryant. 1985. Young children's use of spatial coordinates. *Child Development.* 56 (3): 604–613.

Spectorm, I. 1990. *Rhythm and life: The work of Emile Jacque-Dalcroze.* New York: Stuyvesant Press.

Sperling, G. B. 2005. The case for universal basic education for the world's poorest boys and girls. *Phi Delta Kappan.* 87 (3): 213–216.

Strachey, J. C., ed. 1961. *Standard edition of the complete psychological works of Sigmund Freud.* London: Hogarth Press.

Stuart, M., Dixon, M., and Masterson, J. 1998. Learning to read at home and school. *The British Journal of Educational Psychology.* 68: 3.

Suarez-Orozco, M. M. 2005. Rethinking education in the global era. *Phi Delta Kappan.* 87 (3): 209–212.

Swart, H. W. 1967. *Margarethe Meyer Schurz.* Watertown, WI: The Watertown Historical Society.

Temple, A. 1920. The kindergarten primary unit. *Elementary School Journal.* 20 (April): 498–627.

Terman, L. M. 1919. *The intelligence of school children.* Boston: Houghton Mifflin.

Tharp, L. H. 1950. *The Peabody sisters of Salem.* Boston: Little, Brown and Co.

Thoreau, H. D. 1968. *Walden and the essay on civil disobedience.* New York: Lancer Books.

Uzgiris, I. C. 1981. Two functions of imitation during infancy. *International Journal of Behavioral Development.* 4: 1–12.

Uzgiris, I. C., and McV. Hunt. 1973. *Infant development from a Piagetian approach: Introduction to a symposium.* Paper presented at the American Psychological Association Convention, Montreal, CA.

Uzgiris, I. C., and McV. Hunt. 1975. *Assessment in infancy.* Urbana, IL: University of Illinois Press.

Valois, R. F., and R. E. McKewon. 1998. Frequency and correlates of fighting and carrying weapons among public school adolescents. *American Journal of Health Behavior.* 22: 8–17.

von Hofe, G. D. 1916. Giving the project method a trial. *School Science and Mathematics.* 16 (9): 763–767.

Vandewalker, N. C. 1907. *The history of kindergarten influences in elementary education. The Sixth Yearbook of the National Society for the Scientific Study of Education, Pt. 2.* Chicago: Public School Publishing Company.

Vernazza, M. 1981. *Complete handbook of kindergarten music lesson plans and activities.* West Nyack, NY: Parker Publishing Company.

Vooijs, M. W., and T. H. A. van der Vort, 1993. Learning about television violence: The impact of a critical viewing curriculum on children's attitudinal judgments of crime series. *Journal of Research and Development in Education.* 26 (3): 133–142.

Vygotsky, L. S. 1978. *Mind in society: The development of higher psychological processes,* ed. M. Cole, V. John-Steiner, S. Scribner, and E. Sauberman. Cambridge, MA: Harvard University Press.

Vygotsky, L. S. 1979. *Mind in society: The development of higher mental processes.* Cambridge, MA: Harvard University Press. (Reprinted from original works in 1930, 1933, and 1935).

Vygotsky, L. S. 1986. *Thought and language.* Cambridge, MA: MIT Press. (Reprinted from original work published in 1934).

Wachs, T. D., I. C. Uzgiris, and McV. Hunt. 1971. Cognitive development in infants of different age levels and from different environmental backgrounds. *Merril Palmer Quarterly.* 17: 283–217.

Waters, E. 1983. The stability of individual differences in infant attachment. Comments on the Thompson, Lamb, and Estes contributions. *Child Development.* 54: 516–520.

Watson, J. B. 1928. *Psychological care of infant and child.* New York: W. W. Norton.

Weber, D. J. 1973. *Foreigners in their native land; historical roots of the Mexican Americans.* Albuquerque, NM: University of New Mexico Press.

Weber, E. 1984. *Ideas influencing early childhood education: A theoretical analysis.* New York: Teachers College Press.

Wellman, B. L. 1932. Some new bases for interpretation of the IQ. *Journal of Genetic Psychology.* 41: 116–126.

Werker, J. F., and J. E. Pegg. 1992. Infant speech perception and phonological acquisition. In *Phonological development: Models, research, implications,* ed. C. A. Ferguson, L. Menn, and C. Stoel-Gammon. Timonium, MD: York Press.

Wickett, M. R. 2000. *Contested Territory: Whites, Native Americans, and African Americans in Oklahoma, 1865–1907.* Baton Rouge, LA: University of Louisiana Press.

Wild, R. 2000. *Raising curious, creative, confident kids: The Pestalozzi experiment in child-based education.* New York: Random House.

Willerman, L., S. H. Broman, and M. Fiedler. 1970. Infant development, preschool IQ, and social class. *Child Development.* 41: 69–77.

Williams, B. 2003. Baa Baa Black Sheep! Itsy Bitsy Spider/Twinkle, Twinkle, Little Star. *School Library Journal.* 51: 103.

Windholtz, G. 1991. Pavlov as a youth. *Integrative Physiological and Behavioral Science.* 26: 51–67.

Woodhull, J. F. 1919. The project method in the teaching of science. *School and Society.* 8 (July): 41–44.

Wortham, S. C. 2001. *Assessment in early childhood education.* Upper Saddle River, NJ: Merrill, Prentice Hall.

Zeitz, D. 1969. *Child welfare: Services and perspectives.* New York: Wiley.

Zhao, Y. 2005. Increasing math and science achievement: The best and the worst of the east and west. *Phi Delta Kappan.* 87 (3): 219–222.

Zigler, E., and S. J. Styfco. 1994. Head Start: Criticisms in a constructive context. *American Psychologist.* 49: 127–132.

Subject Index

157

Name Index

About the Author

Harry Morgan teaches child development, learning theory, and research at the University of West Georgia in Carrollton, and his experiences include teaching at Bank Street College in New York City, and professorships at Ohio University and Syracuse University. He is a graduate of New York University, The University of Massachusetts, and the University of Wisconsin-Madison.